Freedom Train North

Stories of the Underground Railroad in Wisconsin

To Dr. John Holzhueter,
mentor and encourager

My joyful thanks to Ms. Pleasant Rowland for believing in this book from the beginning and to Senator Herbert Kohl for helping to fund these strong, beautiful illustrations. Hats off to the Milton Historical Society and the Wisconsin Sesquicentennial Commission for making it all possible.

JP

Freedom Train North

Stories of
The Underground Railroad
In Wisconsin

Julia Pferdehirt

Illustrations by Jerry Butler

LIVING HISTORY PRESS
MIDDLETON, WISCONSIN 53562
In partnership with the Milton Historical Society
Milton, Wisconsin

Freedom Train North
Stories of the Underground Railroad in Wisconsin

Edited by Diane Barnhart

Designed and desktop-published by
Dave and Neta Jackson
Castle Rock Creative, Inc.

Published by Living History Press
7426 Elmwood Avenue
Middleton, Wisconsin 53562
In partnership with
The Milton Historical Society
Milton, Wisconsin

ISBN: 0-9664925-0-1

JCOX

Dec. 1999

Meet the Author . . .

Like her grandfather before her, Julia Pferdehirt is a storyteller. For her, stories are like windows opening our lives and dreams to each other. She lives in Middleton, Wisconsin, with her husband, Wayne, and daughters, Beth, Becky, and Ruth—her biggest encouragers. After *Freedom Train North*, she'll be writing a mystery story set on the Underground Railroad in Kentucky.

. . . and the Illustrator

Jerry Butler's vision is to "capture the truth of the African-American experience" in his art. He is chair of the Art Department of Madison Area Technical College and recently illustrated *Sweet Words So Brave,* a powerful account of the Harlem Renaissance. Mr. Butler is currently writing and illustrating *Drawings in the Dirt*, using the story of his own life as a young artist in rural Mississippi to unfold the history of African-American art.

Introduction

Between the covers of this book are stories of men, women, and children with dreams of freedom. Each is a true story of the Underground Railroad and the part played by the people of Wisconsin. When a story includes spoken words, those words were actually said or written by these people many years ago. Thoughts and feelings described were also recorded by the people who experienced them. However, when personal accounts were not recorded, you may be asked to imagine how people felt and thought.

Contents

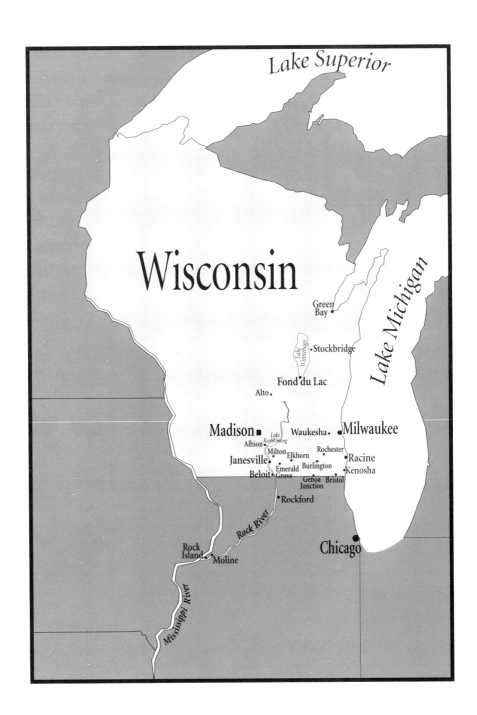

Chapter 1

Freedom Dreams

T he overseer tied me to a tree and flogged me with the whip. . . . While he was eating supper, I got off my shoe, and slipped off a chain and ran."

William Hall had known only slavery from the day he was born until the day that overseer lifted his whip. But that day—that moment—William Hall said, *No more.* He ran for his life. Past dogs and through cold nights, he ran. Sometimes lost and always hungry, he ran. He begged food, slept in the open, and kept running.

He ran north from Tennessee—when

he could find north, that is. Sneaking in the dark through woods and crawling through cornfields turned him in circles. More than once he walked for days in the wrong direction. Where did he find the strength to walk those long miles back again? One night, cold rain wet him to the skin. The next night he hid in a barn, shivering with fever. Shaking, half-starved, and falling-down sick, William Hall made himself go on. Every step was one step closer to freedom.

He reached Illinois. "I got thirty miles out of my way again: so that when I reached Bloomington, I was too tired to go another step," he said. "I found an abolitionist who helped me to Chicago. From about the middle of August to the middle of November, I dwelt in no house except in Springfield. Sick. Had no bed till I got to Bloomington. In February, I cut wood in Indiana. I went to Wisconsin and staid [stayed] till harvest was over; then came to a particular friend."

"Now," his friend said, "square up your business, and go to the lake, for there are men here now, even here where you are living, who would betray you for half a dollar if they knew where your master is. Cross the lake! Get into Canada!"

William Hall's "particular friend" set him on the last miles of his long run to freedom. This friend, and thousands of people like him, called themselves *abolitionists*. Abolitionists worked for the end of slavery. Some spoke out quietly. Some gave speeches or helped slaves run from their so-called masters.

"Cross the lake! Get into Canada!" said William Hall's abolitionist friend. He sent Hall to the shore of Lake Michigan, where steamships set out on the long trip from Kenosha, Racine, or Milwaukee, north through the Straits of Mackinac to Lake Huron's Canadian shore. A few ship captains were secret freedom workers—abolitionists who would smuggle any runaway to Canada, where slavery was outlawed, and black people were free.

It was in Canada—a free man at last—that William Hall told his story in 1856, six years before Abraham Lincoln signed the Emancipation Proclamation.

The Underground Railroad, was it really *under the ground*? History says people running from slavery rode on this railroad to Canada. Just how did that happen?

The Underground Railroad wasn't a railroad at all. There were no steam engines or tracks from one town to the next. What history calls the Underground Railroad was just people, freedom workers scattered all over North America who helped other people escape from slavery.

In some places, freedom workers organized schedules and stops like a real railroad. In other places, like Wisconsin, a few known and trusted friends worked together to help fugitive slaves.

As time passed, the Underground Railroad grew. Codes

were sometimes used to keep their work secret. A safe house was sometimes called a "station." Workers were "conductors." An escaping person might be called "cargo" or a "parcel," another word for package. If a message came saying, "Three parcels due Tuesday," freedom workers expected three people in need of help and hope.

Workers on the Underground Railroad in Wisconsin were just like the people in your town. They were old and young, rich and poor, black, white, and American Indian. They were pastors, farmers, shopkeepers, steamboat captains, and homemakers. Their "stations" were barns and cabins, a tunnel, and once, even an empty sugar barrel!

Fugitive slaves took their freedom into their own hands. They said, *No more.* No more whips and chains. No more masters. No more seeing human beings bought and sold.

Because slavery was legal in the South and illegal in northern states, at first enslaved people ran north. Hungry, cold, and tired to the bone, they were chased by bounty hunters and bloodhounds. The road to freedom was hard. People hid in swamps, waded streams, and swam rivers. By day and in the middle of the night, over city streets and across wide, lonely prairies, they ran. Some ran alone. Others were helped by the Underground Railroad.

In 1850, the Fugitive Slave Law was passed. It allowed slave catchers to capture runaways in any state—even in free states like Wisconsin—and drag them back to slavery.

Freedom Dreams

The law also punished anyone who helped fugitive slaves.

The only hope for freedom then was to leave the United States, so people followed their freedom dreams to Canada. In Canada slavery was outlawed, slave catchers were put in prison, and black people were free citizens.

Thousands of men, women, and children fled through Michigan and crossed the Detroit River. Others walked mile after mile, through New York or Ohio. Still others followed the great Mississippi River or the shore of Lake Michigan. For some of them, the road to freedom passed through the new, wide-open land of Wisconsin. This is their story.

Chapter 2

Independence Day

On July 4, 1842, while all St. Louis, Missouri, celebrated with picnics and parades, 16-year-old Caroline Quarles declared her own Independence Day. She took $100 and a box of clothes and ran for the Mississippi River—and freedom.

Caroline darted along side roads and down alleys to downtown St. Louis. Her running feet beat a rhythm on the wooden sidewalks. She dodged horses and people to reach the Mississippi River docks. There, as she slipped into the crowd of riverboat passengers,

Independence Day

Caroline's light skin and brown hair were her only disguise. Would people think she was a white girl on an afternoon outing? She could only hope.

In 1842 the Mississippi River was like a highway with riverboats headed north and south. A few dollars bought Caroline a ticket across to the free state of Illinois. There she boarded a stagecoach and rode to the end of the line, 400 miles from her master, Charles Hall. The coach bumped and swayed and shook its way north to Wisconsin Territory and the city of Milwaukee.

Milwaukee was new and rough compared to St. Louis. Wooden sidewalks stretched in front of brick and wooden buildings, and the streets smelled of people, horses, and taverns. But in St. Louis, Caroline was a slave—property—just like Master Hall's high-stepping horses. In Wisconsin she was free. Caroline stepped from the stagecoach into another world. Another life.

A barber in Milwaukee's tiny community of free blacks and former slaves offered Caroline a place to stay until she found a job. Caroline and hard work were old friends. In slavery she had done everything from fancy lacework to scrubbing floors. Then, reward posters appeared.

Runaway Slave!
Caroline Quarles, Age 16
$300 Reward

Three hundred dollars! Caroline's barber friend saw the posters. He had once been a slave. He wouldn't betray Caroline, would he? Still, that reward was a magnet. Three hundred dollars was a year's pay. He'd be rich. In the end, the barber traded his self-respect for that $300 by telling slave catchers where Caroline was hidden. Like hounds after a fox, they rushed to Milwaukee to find her.

The slave catchers were quick and clever. They planned to snatch Caroline and run. Couldn't someone stop them? Surely, Milwaukee's abolitionists wouldn't let a young girl be returned to slavery. Wouldn't someone raise a fist and shout, Stop! Kidnappers? Yes, but it would be too late. The plan was intended to work so quickly that by the time freedom-loving people heard the news, Caroline would be back scrubbing floors in Master Hall's fine house, and the slave catchers would be counting reward money.

The plan would have been as smooth as ice on a pond but for one young abolitionist, Asahel Finch. By accident, Finch heard about a runaway slave staying in a barber's shack near the river. He heard the name Caroline Quarles. He heard about slave catchers from St. Louis and knew someone must stop them. Mr. Finch realized he had to be that someone—there was no time to waste.

Armed with nothing but courage, the young freedom worker dashed to the barber's house. The slave catchers could show up at any minute. He had to convince Caroline to run; somehow he had to make her believe she'd been betrayed.

What did he say? Why did she trust him? No one knows. But he did convince her—and not a second too soon. Caroline bundled up her few possessions and followed Finch toward the river just minutes before the barber returned, bringing the slave catchers with him.

The slave catchers searched the barber's house. Empty! Where was that girl? Fighting mad, they threw the barber to the ground. Then, the hunt began. House by house they searched, pounding on doors, yelling, and demanding to know where Caroline was hidden.

While the slave catchers searched, Caroline and Finch crawled along behind brush and weeds. Loud, angry shouts filled the air. How long before they were discovered?

Caroline and Finch decided she must hide. But where? The neighborhood was poor, with houses no bigger than chicken coops. No cellars or attics. Desperately, they looked for a hiding place while the slave catchers' voices grew louder and closer.

Suddenly, they spied an old wooden sugar barrel half-hidden by weeds. The barrel belonged to a black man. Could they use it? Could the man be trusted? With the slave catchers closing in, they had to take a chance.

Mr. Finch pried the lid from the barrel and stuffed

Caroline inside, skirts and all! She could hardly move. Bang! He pounded the lid back on. Then he ran for help, leaving Caroline behind, alone.

Hour after hour on that sizzling August day, Caroline huddled inside the barrel. Imagine the cramping muscles and the smell of sweat and heat and rotting wood. How long could she stay squeezed inside a barrel? Every minute must have crawled by. What could she do? If Mr. Finch didn't come for her, the slave catchers would.

Past midnight, Caroline heard footsteps and voices. Someone was coming! She could not see. Imagine hearing the screech of rusty nails as the barrel was pried open and hoping, *hoping* the people outside were friends. Imagine the barrel's lid lifting. Had Mr. Finch brought help, or were slave catchers waiting?

It was Mr. Finch! His face must have been as welcome as water in a desert. Caroline was safe—for the moment, at least.

There, in the middle of the night on that Milwaukee street, Caroline Quarles' journey on the Underground Railroad began. She hid first at the Browns' farm just outside Milwaukee. Then abolitionists took her 30 miles away near Prairieville (now called Waukesha) to Samuel and Lucinda Daugherty's house.

For three weeks Caroline hid with the Daughertys. The slave catchers set up headquarters at Jones' Tavern in

Prairieville and continued searching. They rode from town to town, bullying, threatening, and bribing. Hired spies watched every crossroad and bridge between Prairieville and Milwaukee. Meanwhile, freedom workers waited. Silence and secrecy were their best weapons.

With a $300 reward posted, it seemed like half the county tried to find Caroline Quarles, and the other half tried to keep her free. Years later, people remembered bounty hunters searching the whole countryside, "armed with pistols, whiskey, and warrants."

The slave catchers tried every trick. They spread lies, saying Caroline wanted to go home, but the abolitionists wouldn't let her. We just want to help a poor girl, they claimed. The slave catchers promised to give her freedom papers. They promised, but few people believed them.

Weeks passed. Caroline stayed hidden, but each day the slave catchers got closer. Then, late one afternoon, they stomped right up onto Samuel and Lucinda Daugherty's front porch! Caroline dashed to the cellar.

The only way out was a potato chute, a narrow, slippery opening from the cellar to the outdoors. She had not come so far to give up! Caroline squeezed up the chute, pushing, pulling, and scrambling to the outside. Then, dragging her long skirts through the dirt, she crawled between rows of corn to the far end of a field and hid. Although the slave catchers searched until dark, they did not find her. Still, Caroline and her abolitionist friends knew she could not hide in cornfields forever. Something must be done.

The answer was clear: Caroline must go to Canada. But the question was *how*? Usually fugitive slaves escaped by ship, but bounty hunters hoping for that $300 reward swarmed like flies around every dock from Kenosha to Milwaukee.

First, two freedom workers, Deacon Ezra Mendall and Lyman Goodnow, volunteered to smuggle Caroline out of Prairieville. Ezra Mendall wasn't afraid of anything or anyone. As a young man, he had brawled and gambled and fought barehanded. In 1842 he was 60 years old and a church deacon, but even that hadn't settled him down. When slave catchers came to his farm looking for Caroline, he ran them off at gunpoint.

Lyman Goodnow was a man who finished what he started. He hated slavery and had no wife or children depending on him. So one night, with a borrowed horse and wagon, the two men stowed Caroline under straw in the back of the wagon and left Prairieville. Where were they headed? "Someplace safe," was all they knew.

All night the wagon bumped and jostled along the roads to Spring Prairie. Two brothers agreed to hide Caroline until Lyman Goodnow returned for her. Caroline was afraid. More strangers. More white faces. She looked at Mr. Goodnow with worry in her eyes. "Am I among friends?" she asked.

Driving back, Mr. Goodnow felt something under the seat. He reached down to find the biggest, sharpest, pig-sticking knife he had ever seen. "Deacon, what is *this*?" he yelled.

"Oh, just something I brought along to pick my teeth with," said the Deacon with a sly smile. If slave catchers had tried to take Caroline, Ezra Mendall was prepared to fight.

Back in Prairieville, worries and plans filled the next days to the brim. Years later Lyman Goodnow wrote, "The more we talked, the more fearful we were she

would be found. Finally, we decided that one of us should go and take the girl through to some station on the Underground Railroad. They pitched upon me, being an old bachelor with no family to do the job."

Goodnow wrote, "I rode to Deacon Edmund Clinton's and said I wanted his saddle, bridle, and all the money he had. I told him, 'I am going on a skeerup, and I may be obliged to pay the Queen a visit before I get back. . . .' He handed me five dollars, all the money he had by him. That made eight dollars."[3]

The "skeerup" to "pay the Queen a visit" was, of course, a trip to Canada, where Queen Victoria of England ruled. With $8 and a borrowed horse, Lyman Goodnow returned to Spring Prairie for Caroline. Freedom workers offered help and money. One man loaned his horse and another gave a wagon and harness. That night, with $20, a pillowcase filled with food, and a letter asking for help from any abolitionist, Goodnow started for Canada—500 miles away—with Caroline buried under hay and a buffalo robe in the back of the wagon.

They drove south to Illinois, around Chicago, through Indiana, and up into Michigan, hiding by day and traveling at night. They stayed in claim shanties, grand houses, and Quaker settlements. Sometimes, rain drenched them. Black, moonless nights and twisting roads confused them. Often hungry and exhausted and always on the lookout for slave catchers, they followed the Underground Railroad from station to station to the Detroit River in Michigan. Even there, reward posters for Caroline had been posted, and a slave catcher from St. Louis prowled the docks. Freedom workers hired a ferryboat to cross the river.

When Caroline stepped from that boat, she cried with joy. Canada! Freedom! She could come and go, think and feel, dream and choose her own way. Since that Independence Day in St. Louis, Caroline Quarles had traveled more than 1,000 miles on the Underground Railroad, from July until October of 1842. She had run from slave catchers, crouched in a sugar barrel, and crawled through a cornfield. She had slept on dirt floors, feather beds, and buried under hay. At last, at long last she had reached Canada. For the first time in her life, she was free.

Caroline Quarles stayed in Canada. She learned to read and write, married a widower named Allen Watkins, and had six children: Marian, William, Marcilin, Mary, Charles, and a baby whose name we do not know. Life was hard, but freedom was precious. In 1880, she wrote her dear friend, Lyman Goodnow.

The beginning of that letter appears on the following page along with a picture of Caroline.

1880
Sandwich, April 17th

Dearest friend: pen and ink could hardly express my joy when I heard from you once more.

I am living and have to work very hard; but I have never forgotten you nor your kindness. I am still in Sandwich–the same place where you left me. Just as soon as the postmaster read the name to me–your name–my heart filled with joy and gladness. . . . Dearest friend, you don't know how rejoiced I feel since I heard from you. Answer this as soon as you get it and let me know how you are, and your address. . . .

Chapter 3

Strong against Slavery

Imagine. You're reading late by the kerosene lamp while a snowstorm blows and wails outside. You hear a knock at the door. Who could it be? With the next farm three miles away, folks don't come calling in the middle of the night. Someone must be in trouble.

"Open up," a voice whispers. "Hurry!"

You put down your book and pull the door latch. Two men rush inside, stomping snow from their feet and slamming the door behind them. Thick woolen scarves hide their faces.

The taller man pulls his scarf away. It's Dr. Strong from Beloit! What is he doing out in this storm?

The second man turns to warm his hands at the pot-bellied stove. "I'm here to ask for your help. I know you can be trusted," says Dr. Strong. "Let me introduce you to Mr. Isaac James."

Mr. James turns from the stove. One look at his face tells you why Dr. Strong is out in a snowstorm in the middle of the night. Isaac James's skin is smooth and dark. Rich, deep brown. His eyes look tired and afraid. A runaway slave has come to your door.

"We need help," Dr. Strong says. "Captain Kilsey's ship, the *Chesapeake,* docks in Racine come Monday. Kilsey will take Isaac to Canada. Will you hide Isaac and take him to meet the *Chesapeake*?"

You have always spoken against slavery. Now, you have the chance to stand behind your words. Will you? Of course. The question is *can* you? You sort through your mind for hiding places and back-road routes to Racine and realize you can't do this alone. You wonder. Who will help? Who can be trusted?

———

This story is imaginary. Only Dr. Strong and Captain Kilsey of the *Chesapeake* are real. But between 1840 and

1862, in big cities, tiny towns, and prairie cabins, Wisconsin freedom workers did ask, Who will help? Who can be trusted?

They trusted close friends or family members, someone at church or an abolitionist neighbor. One by one, names were added to the small list of Wisconsin freedom workers. A network grew that became part of the Underground Railroad. In time people running from slavery could travel from town to town to Lake Michigan.

Prairieville, now called Waukesha, gives us a good picture of Wisconsin's Underground Railroad. Most Prairieville freedom workers belonged to the First Congregational Church. Remember when Lyman Goodnow needed a horse? He didn't go to a stranger; he asked his brother-in-law. Samuel and Lucinda Daugherty hid Caroline Quarles in their house. Down in Wauwatosa, their daughter and her preacher husband helped fugitive slaves, too. And so the network grew.

Were all Wisconsin people abolitionists? No. William Hall's "particular friend" warned him about people who would "betray you for half a dollar." Even in freedom-loving Prairieville, the Daughertys' neighbor tried to turn Caroline over to slave catchers.

Feelings about slavery were strong in Wisconsin. Abolitionist newspapers were published in Racine, Prairieville, and Milwaukee. Sherman Booth, editor of *The Wisconsin*

Freeman, spent a year in jail for helping a runaway slave.

Arguments about slavery exploded like dynamite. In newspaper columns, on street corners, and in the state legislature, people argued for or against slavery. This is the South's problem, not ours, some people thought. If one person isn't free, then no one is truly free, others thought.

Some people fought slavery. Edward Mathews was a Baptist missionary who preached for God and against slavery all over Wisconsin for 20 years. When his missionary society accepted donations from Southern slave owners, Mathews was furious. He refused his pay, saying he would never take a penny of slavers' money.

Other people were pro-slavery. They ridiculed abolitionists and threw anti-slavery preachers like Mathews out of their churches.

Still other people were "fair-weather" abolitionists. In 1842 James Mitchell, chaplain to the Wisconsin legislature, said he was against slavery. All the time, he actually kept two women as slaves. Abolitionists were shocked. He was breaking the law! Set them free, or lose your job, they said. Reverend Mitchell knew slavery was outlawed in Wisconsin, but he wanted to keep his slaves *and* his job. He boldly told everyone he didn't own a single slave—they belonged to his wife! Finally, Mitchell secretly sent the two women to Virginia.

Wisconsin's freedom workers weren't many in number,

but they stood strongly against slavery. Fifteen years after slavery ended, Lyman Goodnow wrote about his own town of Prairieville.

"We were very radical in our views of right and wrong," he wrote. "We opposed bad men everywhere; supported all fugitive slaves who came to us, and worked like beavers for the right."[4] These proud words could have been said about every freedom worker in Wisconsin.

Lyman Goodnow was right; Wisconsin abolitionists were "radical." Once those radical freedom workers even became freedom *fighters* in a true story about a fugitive slave, a battering ram, a jailbreak, and 1,000 angry abolitionists. It all began in far-away Missouri with a man named Joshua Glover.

Chapter 4

Jailbreak!

I n 1854, an anti-slavery storm rolled across Wisconsin. Newsboys hawked Sherman Booth's abolitionist paper, *The Wisconsin Free Democrat*, on street corners, and steamship captains smuggled runaway slaves from Lake Michigan ports to Canada. Then one spring night, slave catchers crept over the state line, and the people of Milwaukee and Racine had to take a stand for freedom.

In Missouri a man named Joshua Glover had decided to "steal himself" from his master, Benami Garland. He ran and kept running until he reached Racine, Wisconsin, hundreds of miles away. In Racine, Glover found a job at the Rice and Sinclair Mill. He worked hard, saving money for land and a house. As he settled along the Root River, Joshua Glover did more than buy himself a home, he was building a whole new life.

By 1854, nearly three years later, Glover was settled and happy. One Saturday evening he sat laughing and playing cards with three friends when, suddenly, someone pounded on the door. Open in the name of the law! It was U.S. Marshal Charles Cotton with a warrant for Joshua Glover's arrest!

Glover jumped up. An arrest warrant could mean only one thing—slave catchers. What could he do? Even in free Wisconsin, the law was not on his side. He had seen other runaways put in chains and taken back to slavery.

Glover had one small hope. The door was latched. Maybe he could slip out the window and disappear into the woods.

Before Glover could reach the window, one of his friends, Nelson Turner, did an unbelievable, unthinkable thing. He pulled the latch and unlocked the door!

Crash! The door flew open. In seconds, the cabin was filled with yelling and fighting. U.S. Marshal Cotton and his men pushed their way inside, followed by bounty-hunting slave catchers, a police officer from St. Louis, and the last face Joshua Glover ever wanted to see again—his master, Benami Garland.

Glover raised his fists to fight. But what could he do against swinging clubs and iron handcuffs? The men kicked and beat Glover and threw him, bleeding and half-conscious, in the back of their wagon. The driver shouted to the horses and flicked the whip. Later, people spread the story that Nelson Turner received $100, blood money for betraying his friend.

U.S. Marshal Cotton and his men knew abolitionists in Racine would not stand by and watch a free citizen dragged back to slavery. They decided to drive Joshua Glover secretly to Milwaukee. Their plan was to hold him in jail, find a pro-slavery judge to sign the legal papers, and whisk him back to Missouri. Speed and darkness were on their side. No one and nothing seemed to be on Joshua Glover's side.

Marshal Cotton and the slave catchers made one mistake, however. They forgot the people in Milwaukee who loved freedom. The Fugitive Slave Law of 1850 made it a crime to help a runaway slave, and the slave catchers did not believe anyone would break the law for one black man.

By the next morning, news of Joshua Glover

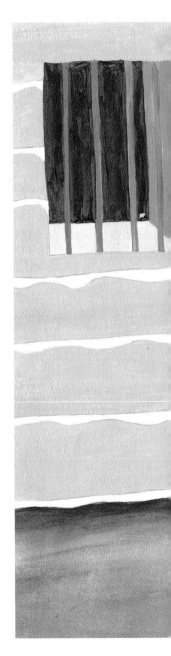

flashed through Milwaukee. People were outraged. A fugitive slave jailed in their city? Sherman Booth jumped on a horse and tore up and down the streets of Milwaukee like another Paul Revere. He shouted for people to assemble at the jail. Church bells began to ring from every corner of the city. A loud, angry crowd gathered. Release this man now! people demanded. Speeches were given, and pistols fired into the air. Wisconsin was a free state, and these people weren't willing to let anything—even the Fugitive Slave Law—change that. With every hour, the crowd grew larger and louder and angrier.

Down in Racine, news of Joshua Glover's arrest spread like a prairie fire, hot and quick. If Racine's abolitionists had anything to say about it, Joshua Glover would not go back to slavery without a fight.

One hundred men rushed on board the steamship *Pacific*, headed for Milwaukee. There was not a minute to waste. If they didn't reach Milwaukee in time, they feared Joshua Glover would already be taken away. Men whipped off their jackets and grabbed shovels. In the breath-stealing heat below deck, they fed coal into the ship's boilers. Every minute counted. They had to reach Milwaukee in time.

When the *Pacific* pulled to the Milwaukee shore, the Racine men stampeded down the docks to the Milwaukee jail. There, to their amazement, they found more than 1,000 people shouting for the release of Joshua Glover.

U.S. Marshal Cotton was in a terrible fix. His job was to enforce the Fugitive Slave Law, but the crowd outside the jail was growing bigger and wilder by the minute. The Racine men arrived with legal papers demanding that Joshua Glover be sent back to Racine. The papers even included arrest warrants charging Benami Garland and Marshal Cotton with assault for beating Joshua Glover.

Marshal Cotton did not see any way out. The Fugitive Slave Law was the law of the whole country. By that law, Joshua Glover wasn't a citizen with rights; he was Mr. Benami Garland's property, no different from a runaway dog. It was Marshal Cotton's job to make sure that "property" was returned. He must enforce the law!

The crowd roared. Fists pounded the air. What kind of law made slave catchers out of people who hated slavery? Some laws, people said, were better broken.

The crowd pushed and shoved outside the jail. Set him free! they demanded. They wouldn't be slave catchers for anyone! One man ran up with a pickax. Others brought a log nearly 20 feet long. The crowd had talked and listened long enough. The Fugitive Slave Law was not the only thing about to be broken!

The heavy log became a battering ram. Boom! Again and again the men slammed it against the jail door. Crack! The pickax struck the wood. The door splintered, then was pulled to pieces. Abolitionists pushed toward the jail. Free Joshua Glover! they demanded. Marshal Cotton's men tried to push them back. The street was a battlefield.

All around, people shouted and pushed. The marshal's men threatened to shoot. Would someone die before Joshua Glover could be freed? The crowd pressed closer.

Like a tidal wave, people surrounded Joshua Glover. Strong arms pushed Marshal Cotton and his men away. The crowd poured onto Wisconsin Street, down East Water Street, and rumbled to a stop at Walker's Point Bridge. There, Glover was tossed into the back of John Messenger's wagon. "Drive, Messenger! Drive!" someone yelled. As the wagon tore down the street, police officers, Marshal Cotton's men, slave catchers, and even Benami Garland chased after. Folks said later that it looked like the entire U.S. government running down the middle of the road.

John Messenger drove clear to Waukesha before he pulled his exhausted horses to a stop and Joshua Glover could finally raise his head. Glover did not realize it then, but he was about to climb aboard the Underground Railroad, headed to freedom.

During the next few days, slave catchers and the Underground Railroad played a dangerous game of hide-and-seek. Marshal Cotton and his men waved arrest warrants around like flags. Where is Glover? they demanded. Sherman Booth and other abolitionists were thrown in jail, and free black people were threatened.

Meanwhile, the Underground Railroad set about its silent and secret work. Joshua Glover spent the first night in the Tichnors' barn in Waukesha. Hiding by day and traveling only at night, he moved to Richard Ela's shop in Rochester and then to Reverend and Mrs. Kinney's house in Racine. No one knows how many people hid Glover.

While the slave catchers threatened and hunted, the Underground Railroad waited and watched. Then one night, a steamship with an abolitionist captain arrived in Racine harbor. Glover climbed into the back of a wagon, and an abolitionist friend drove to the docks. They kept in the shadows until Joshua Glover could sneak on board the ship.

Before morning, the great paddle wheel began to turn, and

Joshua Glover. Photo courtesy of the State Historical Society of Wisconsin, Madison.

the steamship, with her precious, hidden cargo, set off for Canada. Joshua Glover's final miles on the Underground Railroad had begun.

———

Joshua Glover finally did reach Canada and freedom. But back in Wisconsin, his rescue lit a wildfire. Sherman Booth was convicted of breaking the Fugitive Slave Law for his part in Glover's escape. He was fined $2,460—about five year's pay!

When the federal judge declared Sherman Booth guilty, Wisconsin's Supreme Court declared him innocent. The Wisconsin judges rejected the Fugitive Slave Law because it denied people a fair trial.

The federal court said Wisconsin must accept and enforce the Fugitive Slave Law. Again, Wisconsin's judges refused. The whole country watched in amazement as the new state of Wisconsin defied the federal government.

Finally in 1861, President Buchanan pardoned Sherman Booth. Once Booth was freed—after spending time in and out of jail while his case was disputed—he became part of the Republican Party, the party that nominated Abraham Lincoln for President.

Chapter 5

Secret Service

More than 150 years ago, Eliza and Jeremiah Porter were missionaries in the small settlement of Green Bay. Winters were fierce, food was scarce, and life was tough as old leather. As the biggest town for miles around, Green Bay was not much more than a few streets with houses and a busy harbor hanging on the edge of Lake Michigan. The highest view in town, from the bell tower of the Porters' church, showed miles of woods and water on every side. Still, Green Bay must have seemed as grand as

New York City to the trappers and traders who came out of the forest once or twice a year, hauling piles of furs to swap for food or money.

The Porters' door was always open to anyone sick, hungry, or just worn thin with loneliness after months and months of winter. So the Porters were not surprised when a letter arrived from the Stockbridge Indians announcing some unusual visitors.

The Stockbridge were a proud people living on the eastern shore of Lake Winnebago. They had been forced from their lands in Massachusetts and New York by the U.S. government. The letter said they had hidden a family of fugitive slaves, a desperate father and two young children. Where was their mother? No one knew. Slavery is cruel. She may have died or even been sold away.

Wherever people ran from slavery, slave catchers were always a danger, so the Stockbridge kept watch. Sure enough, bounty hunters were spotted sneaking around Stockbridge land; the family was no longer safe. The presence of slave catchers in the area meant work for the Underground Railroad. So a letter was sent to Green Bay, and the freedom train began to "move."

Eliza Chappell Porter told the story in a letter to her daughter. She wrote, "A letter came from Mr. Goodell of Stockbridge saying that a father and his children had for some time enjoyed refuge in that Indian nation, but pursuers had discovered their resting place. . . . Would we receive them and send them to the steamboat on the coming Tuesday? Surely we could do that. . . ."[5]

Would the Porters help? Of course. They knew Captain Stewart of the fine ship *Michigan* would take any fugitive slave to Canada. What could be simpler than hiding a family overnight and sneaking them on board a waiting ship? However, the Porters soon learned that when slave catchers, reward money, and freedom were involved, nothing was simple.

"They did not arrive at the hour appointed," Mrs. Porter wrote. "But at midnight we were awakened by a knock at our window, and there stood the poor trembling father and his cold, hungry children. Our house was already full and the boat was not in port, and they feared the pursuers were on their track."[6]

The Porters welcomed the family with hot food and a warm fire. Their sad, hard story tumbled out as the Porters listened.

Somewhere in the South this father had stolen away with his three children. On foot they managed to avoid betrayers, bloodhounds, and bounty hunters until they reached St. Louis, Missouri. Eliza and Jeremiah listened in horror as the father unfolded his grief. One child grew sick. Nothing the desperate man could do made any difference; his little one just grew sicker and sicker until the child died.

There was no time for tears. Slave catchers would not wait for them to grieve, so he had to bury his child and keep running. Somehow they covered the long miles to Wisconsin and found safety and kindness with the Stockbridge people. But even there, slave catchers found them, and they had to run again.

Mrs. Porter wondered what to do. The house was full, and other guests were expected. "Where can we hide them?" she wondered. "In the ice-house? In the side closets of the parsonage? I asked the God of all wisdom, love, and truth to direct."

The answer came like a lightning flash. "That is the place!" Mr. Porter replied. "The belfry!"[7]

Before the first morning sunlight, Eliza gathered food and blankets, and Jeremiah took the family to the church. Silently they crept inside and began to climb the narrow ladder to the bell tower. Higher and higher they climbed until they pushed open a trap door to a tiny room at the very top. They could see all Green Bay from this treetop perch—streets and houses, kitchen gardens, shops, and barns. In the distance they saw the smokestacks of steamships and the docks where they hoped and prayed the *Michigan* would come to port.

But the *Michigan* did not come. Days of whispering and nights of waiting passed without a single sign of Captain Stewart or his ship. The lake was a dangerous place; storms

and fire had sunk steamers many times before. What would the Porters do if the *Michigan* never arrived? Every freedom worker in Green Bay was watching that dock.

Time must have passed so slowly. Hour after hour the children had to be as silent as stones. No one must suspect that people were hiding in the bell tower. Thursday, Friday, and Saturday passed, and the Porters began to worry about a new problem. Sunday morning the bell would ring, and the church would fill with people. What would the family do then?

The question was answered by good news! At last, the steamer *Michigan* had been spotted heading into Green Bay harbor. Every freedom worker jumped into action. Deacon Kimball made tracks to Captain Stewart with a message that three extra passengers would be boarding. The Porters quietly led the father and children to the river where an abolitionist friend rowed them out to the waiting ship.

From there the Porters said, "Captain Stewart took them into his care." The steamship puffed its way north across Lake Michigan to Lake Huron, "to her Majesty's land of freedom": Canada. On the Canadian shore the grateful father fell on his knees to "kiss the free soil and give thanks to the Lord who had brought them out of the house of bondage."[8]

Secret Service

This story is especially interesting because European-American and American Indian abolitionists worked together. This had happened before. Once Stockbridge, Brothertown, and white neighbors met to start an anti-slavery society. One Stockbridge man named Collins Fowler said he was willing to die to see slavery ended. "Whatever others thought," Reverend Edward Mathews wrote, "he was willing to testify against slavery, even if for doing so his life should be sacrificed." At the meeting a black man rose to speak. He had been a slave until he found safety with the Brothertown tribe. In front of everyone he cried for his brothers and sisters still in slavery.

All abolitionists were courageous, but American Indian freedom workers were especially brave. With the government pushing tribes onto reservations, they risked even more trouble by protecting runaway slaves. The names Stockbridge and Brothertown have places of honor in the history of Wisconsin's Underground Railroad.

Chapter 6

Overground, Underground

Every house in Janesville was still and dark when Hiram and Eliza Foote heard a knock at their door. Since their home was one of the safe places called "stations" on the Underground Railroad, they were always ready for secret, late-night visitors.

Every homesteader in the county knew Hiram Foote as a pioneer preacher. He and Eliza moved from place to place, preaching in someone's barn one Sunday and a one-room cabin the next until folks scraped up enough money to put up a church building.

Overground, Underground

What people did not know was that while Hiram and Eliza built churches in the newborn towns of Wisconsin territory, they were also building stations and networks of workers on the Underground Railroad. So that night in Janesville, the Footes were not surprised to open their door to someone on the run from slavery—someone alone, afraid, and leaning on a crutch. His name was George.

Forty years later, Eliza Foote wrote down George's story. Somewhere between Illinois and the Wisconsin border, slave catchers had shot him as he fled. Bleeding and in pain, he somehow limped and crawled to an Underground Railroad station. Freedom workers cut the bullet from his leg, bandaged it, and hurried him on to the Footes' house as soon as he could walk. Time was precious because the slave catchers would not give up looking. They had shot him once and wouldn't hesitate to shoot again.

"Three lawyers who could be trusted came under cover of darkness for fear of pro-slavery laws, to interview our guest," Eliza wrote. Hiram and Eliza needed to be sure this man was truly a fugitive slave. Slave catchers would do anything for reward money. Someone might even pretend to be a runaway in order to betray freedom workers and hurt the Underground Railroad. But George was no betrayer; he was a brave man desperate for freedom.

After weeks on the run, George needed sleep as much

as food and bandages, so he stayed with the Footes for two days. Then, Eliza explained, "He was fed, clothed, and provided with a satchel [suitcase] that he might appear more like a northern tourist than a runaway slave." Dressed like a gentleman, who would guess that George was running from slavery? He would look like a freedman visiting relatives in Milwaukee or Racine. With this disguise, he went on to the lake where a steamship waited.

Even on board an abolitionist's ship George was not completely safe. Hiram and Eliza would worry until he was free in Canada. So, as George left, Hiram handed him an envelope addressed to the Reverend and Mrs. Hiram Foote, Janesville, Wisconsin USA, to be mailed when he arrived in Canada. Then, they waited, hoping for good news. "In due time," Eliza wrote, the letter came, "which meant as much to us as though containing an account of the journey. We knew George was safe."

Hiram and Eliza Foote were church leaders in the Wisconsin towns of Janesville, Racine, Emerald Grove, Milton, and Waukesha. Everywhere Hiram preached the same, simple message: love God, help your neighbor, and stand like a rock against slavery. It was no accident that *each* of these places was a stop on Wisconsin's Underground Railroad.

Overground, Underground

A half-day's wagon ride from Janesville is the little pioneer town of Milton. In Milton today people can still see a most unusual station on Wisconsin's Underground Railroad, the Milton House Inn.

In 1819 Joseph Goodrich hiked into the hills of western New York with a bundle of clothes on his back, an ax in his hand, and 50 cents in his pocket. He and his sweetheart, Nancy Maxson, married and set up housekeeping in a log cabin with a dirt floor and a blanket for a door. Today, movies would make their life look like a romantic adventure. In reality it was endless, weary, sunup-to-sundown, hard work.

The New York land was poor. Their best crop was fieldstones and tree stumps. Then drought settled in. Wheat crumbled in the fields like old paper. So in 1838 Joseph went west to Wisconsin. He had heard about the prairies and great stretches of oak and pine forest. Wisconsin land was cheap and good. If hard work could get them a farm, they would work.

When Joseph returned, the family loaded everything they owned in a wagon, and Nancy, Joseph, their daughter, Jane, and son, Ezra, joined the thousands of pioneers on the road to Wisconsin Territory. They spent the first summer in a one-room house in Milton, Wisconsin, with 13 people packed inside!

A territorial road passed through Milton. Joseph and

Nancy Goodrich figured tired travelers would pay for soft beds and a good supper, so they built an inn. Soon stage-coaches were stopping at the Milton House, and those feather beds were filled with travelers headed to or from the big cities of Milwaukee and Chicago.

The Goodrichs were more than pioneers. They were also Seventh Day Baptists, Christian people of deep faith known from New York to the Mississippi River as rock-solid, no-compromise abolitionists. No penny of slavers' money was welcome in their offering boxes. No slave owners sat in their congregations. Seventh Day Baptists were warriors in the fight against slavery. When the chance came for the Goodrichs to join that fight, they did not hesitate.

Joseph's brother, William, settled in Wisconsin too. He ran a ferry across the Rock River, shuttling wagons, people, and goods. On at least one occasion, he carried a human "parcel," a man named Andrew Pratt who had run from slavery.

Andrew Pratt ran from somewhere in Missouri just before the Civil War. He reached Illinois, thinking he would be safe. After all, Illinois was a free state. Or was it? Pratt did not know about Black Laws written to keep black people without jobs and money from settling in Illinois. Where would a fugitive slave get a job and money? So Andrew Pratt, who had come to Illinois to be free, was thrown in jail for the "crime" of being black!

Overground, Underground

What happened then? Maybe Pratt was taken to the Wisconsin border and released. Maybe he escaped. Maybe abolitionists helped him. No one knows. But, about five years later, Ezra Goodrich, Joseph and Nancy's son, wrote Pratt's story.

"Through the assistance of a noble-hearted Uncle of mine, William Goodrich," Ezra wrote, "Andrew Pratt was brought to the quiet and liberty loving little village of Milton."

Before Andrew Pratt's freedom journey ended, he would reach a most unusual station on the Underground Railroad. William Goodrich brought Pratt to one place he knew people running from slavery were always welcome: his brother Joseph's inn at Milton.

Nancy and Joseph Goodrich never asked *if* they would help fugitive slaves, but *how*. In their tiny town, keeping secrets was hard. In a hotel where people came at any hour, it was almost impossible. How could they have hotel guests upstairs and other—secret—guests in the cellar? Fugitive slaves could not just knock on the hotel door. They needed a secret entrance. Again, the question was *how?*

Joseph Goodrich did not let problems stand in his way. One idea led to another, until he had a bold, wild plan.

Just as the name Underground Railroad suggests, Joseph went *under the ground.* A tiny log cabin stood in back of the inn. Joseph cut a trap door in the cabin floor and

began to dig. He scraped, shoveled, and hauled until he had dug a tunnel 50 feet long and 3 feet high—straight into the cellar of the Milton House Inn!

Andrew Pratt hid in the tunnel. When it was safe, Joseph sent him to a friend who needed a good farmhand. Over the next five years, Pratt went into business for himself. Later, he became a homesteader, plowing acres of prairie grass to "prove up" or pay for government land with hard work instead of money. By 1865 he had won the friendship and respect of many in Milton, including Ezra Goodrich.

Many years later, a torn piece of paper no bigger than a child's hand was found among the Goodrich family letters and diaries. The paper was the final puzzle piece in the story of Andrew Pratt and the Milton House tunnel. The paper read as follows:

"Andrew Pratt came to J . . .
in 1861 was cared for and . . .
the underground passage, . . .
him a job with David Plott . . .
village where he worked & . . . .
Afterwards emigrated to . . .
where he proved up on Gov . . . ."

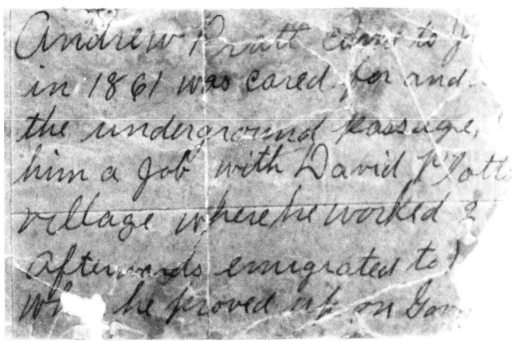

Photo courtesy of the Milton Historical Society, Milton, Wisconsin.

Overground, Underground

The underground tunnel to the cellar of the Milton House Inn still exists and is part of the Milton Historical Society Museum, Wisconsin's only site on the register of National Historic Landmarks of the Underground Railroad.

One hundred fifty years ago, fugitive slaves crawled on hands and knees along a dirt passage barely wider than a man's shoulders. Today the tunnel has stone walls and a cement floor; however, the chilly, underground darkness has not changed. Visitors' hearts still beat faster as they stare through the opening in the cabin floor and creep down the ladder. The darkness gives an unexpected shiver of fear, as though the tunnel itself remembers other long-ago visitors to the Milton House cellar.

Chapter 7

Sketches from the Road

Like sketches, the stories in this chapter are incomplete pictures. History has saved only these bits and pieces, but together, they help tell the whole story.

Hoofin' It to the Lake

In the days of the Underground Railroad, Kenosha was called Southport, *south* because it was near Wisconsin's southern border and *port* because Lake Michigan steamships stopped there. Kenosha was the first Underground

Railroad station along Lake Michigan north of Illinois. Some fugitives made their way around Chicago and trekked north on foot —"hoofin' it." Others followed rivers and dirt roads from the Mississippi River into Wisconsin.

Whole families were freedom workers in Kenosha. Teenagers went on errands with secret "cargo" hidden in the back of the family's wagon. Children took blankets to a hidden guest or filled a basket with food for a hungry runaway. But first, even the youngest child had to learn the silent and secret ways of the Underground Railroad. One woman, Kate Deming, told her childhood story to her son, who wrote it down for us.

There were strange goings-on at little Kate Deming's house. She did not understand why Papa and Mama were whispering. Who were the strangers who came at night and left before breakfast? What was an Underground Railroad?

As she grew, she *did* understand, and she, too, became a freedom worker. Her first job was to keep a secret. She knew about the "guests" in their attic, but she never, never would tell—not even her best friend. People had already plotted to fire her papa from his job for preaching against slavery. If they knew he hid runaways, they would hand him over to the U.S. marshal without a second thought.

"Now Kate," her mother said, "don't tell any of the children at school today about the black man in the attic, or the officers may come and take him away, and they may perhaps put your father into prison."[12]

For two or three days Kate carried the awful, terrifying knowledge that her family was breaking the law by hiding fugitive slaves. When their "guest" finally slipped safely on board a steamship, Kate's whole family must have breathed a sigh of relief.

Some of the Demings' neighbors had secrets of their own. William Smith was a teenager when his father told him, "Don't go the barn tonight. Father will do the chores."[13] William woke in the morning to find his horse tired and the wagon wheels muddy. Yet at breakfast his father smiled and chatted and teased the little ones as though nothing had happened. William was not fooled for a minute. Father had gone somewhere in the middle of the night. Behind his pasted-on smile, he looked worried and tired. What secret was he keeping?

William's answer came weeks later. Night had barely settled in when Mother scooted the little ones to bed and sent William to the kitchen to fix food. Fixing supper at bedtime? Suddenly, the kitchen door opened and four people, a father, mother, and two children, were pushed inside. William did not have to ask who they were; their anxious faces told him everything.

The family stayed only long enough to eat and squeeze into the back of the Smiths' wagon. Without a word, William's father flicked the reins and guided the wagon down the gravel driveway. William watched them disappear into the darkness.

The next morning William came to the breakfast table as usual. He smiled and chatted and teased his little brothers as though nothing had happened.

Kellogg's Tavern

Theodore Fellows had made the trip from Genoa Junction to Kenosha so many times with his father that he could practically drive the roads in his sleep. They always drove all day, slept at James Kellogg's tavern in Bristol, and reached Kenosha the next morning.

Genoa Junction was so small that if the neighbor's pig had a litter, folks considered it major news. Kenosha was a *real* city, with wide streets and long piers stretching like fingers out into Lake Michigan. For Theodore, a trip to Kenosha was a chance to hear real news and see real sights. This time he was going alone.

Theodore loaded hundred-pound bags of wheat into the wagon. The job was a sweaty backbreaker, so he was glad when Father offered to help. But then Father began arranging the bags around the wagon sides with an open square in the center. Theodore stared. What was Father doing?

"It rides better that way," Father explained. Theodore had

loaded wagons since he was old enough to lift a grain sack, and this was the first time Father had done such a thing. Odd.

The next morning the open square was covered with bags of grain. Father handed Theodore his lunch with very particular, unusual instructions. First, he was to eat down by the Fox River. No dawdling. Father said, "Don't speak to anyone unless necessary, and then say nothing but 'yes' and 'no.'"[14] By dark he would reach Kellogg's Tavern.

Imagine. Theodore's father was acting so strangely. First, there was the peculiarly loaded wagon, then the stern looks and instructions to keep quiet. Something was wrong. The best part of a trip was to talk and hear the news from folks along the way, and Father knew it. It all made no sense. Still, Theodore knew better than to question his father, so he obeyed the unusual orders.

That night at the Bristol Tavern, James Kellogg was waiting in the driveway. He signaled the wagon straight into the barn and kicked the door shut. Without a word, Kellogg began to unload the wagon. What was he doing? Then, Theodore was absolutely, completely amazed. Mr. Kellogg pulled a *man* out from under the bags of wheat and hustled him away toward the house.

Suddenly, everything made sense. Father had loaded the wheat and ordered Theodore to keep to himself because a fugitive slave was hidden in the back of the wagon!

Back home in Genoa Junction, Theodore Fellows' father told him about the Underground Railroad. Probably this surprise at Kellogg's Tavern was not the only time the Fellows family made the trip to Kenosha with cargo much more valuable than wheat in the back of their wagon.

James Kellogg was a tough old character who did pretty much as he pleased, and, seemingly, it pleased him to help the fugitive slaves.

—*Images of the Past:* Kenosha Kaleidoscope

Burlington

Dr. Dyer was a "double abolitionist" who not only hid runaways in his home but was a leader in the work against slavery. When Caroline Quarles and Lyman Goodnow needed money for their journey to Canada, Dr. Dyer passed the hat among abolitionists right on the sidewalk in Burlington. He also named the street in front of his house "Liberty Avenue."

Can liberty and slavery long dwell together? Which side shall we be on? Surely we will be for liberty.

—*Dr. Edward Galusha Dyer, Burlington*

Freedom Train North

Alto: On the Prairie

My father kept an underground station. Many a night I have slept out on the prairie with some runaway slaves, with father and the neighbors protecting them against the United States marshal. I found myself, when eighteen years of age, carrying a Sharp's rifle in 1856 with John Brown, in Kansas." —*J.B. Pond, 1900*

Peewaukee: Sleeping by the Stove

I recall . . . an old colored man, carrying a small child, was brought into the house, fed, and put to sleep on the floor near the kitchen stove. During the night my father took a load of hay to some man quite a distance away. Years later my mother told me that the colored man and child were slaves whom my father had smuggled away under cover of the hay to the next station of the 'Underground Railway.' " —*Mollie Maurer Kartak, 1926*

Emerald Grove: Race to Racine

It was a crisp, red-and-gold Wisconsin autumn day in 1855 in the little crossroads town of Emerald Grove.

Deacon and Mrs. Cheney set hot dishes on the table. As the family ate, a covered carriage rumbled up the drive. Sunday visitors, what a surprise! The children tumbled out the door and surrounded the carriage. The rain flaps were lowered to hide the passengers. Even 40 years later, one of those children, Russell Cheney, Jr., remembered what happened next.

Mr. Leonard, a friend from Beloit, jumped from the carriage seat and called out to Deacon Cheney. The children could hardly believe what they heard. Inside the wagon were six fugitive slaves: a husband, wife, and four children. A slave hunter was following close behind!

The Cheney children crowded closer. Were there really runaway slaves in the wagon? While the adults spoke in low, serious tones, the children lifted the rain flaps and peeked inside. Four other children stared back at them.

In another place and time, the children might have become friends. But on that day slavery and slave catchers stood between them.

Deacon Cheney took the reins and sped to the home of a trusted abolitionist friend, Simeon Reynolds. If they left immediately and raced to Racine, they could catch the outgoing steamer and leave the slave hunter empty-handed.

That was exactly what Simeon Reynolds did. For 60 miles Reynolds dodged potholes and mud down the territorial road to the Racine docks. Not long after, freedom workers sent back the "glad news" that the family was safe in Canada.

Chapter 8

Open the Window and Jump!

In 1848, Captain Gillman Appleby of the steamship *Sultana* became a Wisconsin hero. Out on Lake Erie, hundreds of miles from the docks of Racine and Milwaukee, he saved a fugitive slave named Jacob Green.

Jacob Green just would not give up his freedom dreams. Four times he ran from slavery: first from Kentucky; then from New Orleans; a third time from Maryland; and finally, from Kentucky again. He ran from cruel masters and kind ones. He ran from big plantations and riverboats. Each time he was caught. Each time he was whipped and sold. Then, in a new place with a new master, he would pretend to be an obedient slave while keeping his eyes open for a chance to run. When that chance came, north he went again!

Once he rubbed manure on his feet to fool bloodhounds. Another time, with slave catchers in pursuit, he raced through the back door of an Irish family's shanty, across the kitchen, and out the front, knocking the whole family to the floor as he passed. He crawled into a cellar and spent the night squeezed inside a chimney. Still another time he pretended he could not hear or speak. Slave catchers decided he was a madman and let him go. He didn't wait a minute longer than necessary before heading north.

He found help from free blacks on the Underground Railroad. They smuggled him into the dark hold of a Mississippi riverboat where he burrowed under bales of cotton. From boat to wagon, back road to city street, he traveled until he reached Utica, New York. Canada was almost in sight. Almost.

With Canada only a day's journey away, Jacob Green saw a face he had hoped never to see again. His former owner from Kentucky! Green turned to run. The man screamed for help, and a dozen people came running.

Strong arms grabbed Green and held him until police arrived with ankle irons and handcuffs. Jacob Green was caught again and thrown in jail.

"While in prison," Green wrote later, "a complaint was made that a fugitive slave was placed in irons, contrary to the law." News of Green's capture spread. Angry crowds of abolitionists protested outside the jail. "On the Monday following I was taken on board the steamboat *Sultana* bound for Sandusky, Ohio, and on my way there, the Black people in large numbers made an attempt to rescue me. And so desperate was the attack that several officers were wounded, and the attempt failed. I was placed in the cabin."

Locked in and tied up, Jacob Green could only wait, knowing that in a few hours he would be shoved on board a train, chained to the wall, and shipped back to Kentucky.

Gillman Appleby, captain of the *Sultana,* had watched police wrestle Jacob Green on board his ship. He watched as they pushed Green into the captain's cabin. He could not help but hear the crowd roar and shout, demanding Green's release.

Captain Appleby saw it all and did nothing. He stood by while Green was tied up. Just one more uncaring white man, or so it seemed.

Actually, Gillman Appleby cared so much he could have wept, but he could not show it. He had to keep a secret, and nothing—not even Jacob Green's freedom—was more important. The secret? Gillman Appleby was a Wisconsin freedom worker who used his beautiful new ship, the *Sultana*, to smuggle fugitive slaves to Canada.

What could the captain do? Hundreds of miles away in Wisconsin he would have had abolitionist friends nearby and ready to help. But there on the shore of Lake Erie, he was alone.

Alone or not, secret or no secret, Appleby would not let his ship be used for slave catching while he had any power to stop it. He would help; he just needed a chance, a plan, and a bit of luck.

Jacob Green wrote, "At dinner time the steamboat started and had about half a mile to go before she got into the lake, and on the way, the captain came down to me and cautiously asked me if I could swim."[15]

Swim? A person could freeze to death in Lake Erie in the middle of November. No matter. Jacob Green said he could—and would—so the captain untied him.

"He told me to stand close by a window," Green continued. "And when the paddle wheels ceased I must jump out. I stood ready, and as soon as the wheels ceased I made a spring and jumped."[16] Down, down, down, he fell. Freezing water swelled over him. It was bone-aching, heart-stopping cold. Water that cold stabs like needles and sucks the breath from your body. Jacob Green fought his way to the

surface and gasped to pull air into his lungs. Then he began to swim.

Everyone has heard the phrase "run for your life." Well, Jacob Green *swam* for his life. When Captain Appleby saw Green in the water, he gave the signal to start the ship's engines again. Smoke poured from the stacks, and the great paddle wheel began to turn.

In the water, Green had to pull with every ounce of his strength just to keep from being sucked under by the force of the paddles. As he flailed and kicked away from the boat he heard his former owner shout, "Here, here, stop, Captain! Stop!" The man yelled and waved his arms. Soon every person on deck knew a runaway slave was swimming to freedom. Passengers pressed against the railing and shouted as Jacob Green struggled toward shore. If the steamer had stopped, Green would have had no hope, but Captain Appleby did not say a word. By the time Green reached the shore, the *Sultana* was gone.

Jacob Green staggered ashore—shivering, numb, and half-frozen—near Cleveland, Ohio. A crowd of abolitionists hurried him away. But even then his story was not finished.

Before Jacob Green finally became a free man, he was discovered, arrested, and sold once more in Kentucky, back where he had started.

In Kentucky, with a new owner, Green acted like an obedient slave for almost a year. He bowed and smiled and said, "Yes master." But all the time he was waiting for a chance to run.

That chance came one day when Green was ordered to drive his master's daughter to the city. Instead he stopped, tied the young woman to a tree with her own shawl, jumped back in the wagon, and sprinted for the Ohio River. At the river, where black men often worked loading and unloading freight, Green hoisted a trunk onto his shoulder and walked right on board a steamship as if he'd been a dockhand all his life.

Jacob Green made this last escape with the help of the

The *Sultana*, 1847, Gillman Appleby, captain. Photo courtesy of the Buffalo and Erie County Historical Society, Buffalo, New York.

Underground Railroad. To fool slave hunters, freedom workers gave him women's clothes. Wearing long skirts, gloves, and a veil, and carrying $12 in his pocket, he crossed Niagara Falls and headed to Toronto, Canada.

In Toronto, Jacob Green said, at last, "I sang my song of deliverance."[17]

The name Gillman Appleby and the *Sultana* were not alone on Wisconsin's honor role of abolitionist steamship captains and their ships. In 1896, Racine freedom worker A. P. Dutton listed these captains and their floating "stations" on Wisconsin's Underground Railroad.

The *Madison*
The *Niagara*
The *Missouri*
The *Keystone State*
All General Reed's ships
Captain Stewart of the *Michigan*
Captain Steel of the *Galena*
Captain Appleby of the *Sultana*
Captain Kilsey of the *Chesapeake*

A. P. Dutton said more than 100 fugitive slaves were sent to freedom in Canada from the steamer docks in Racine alone. For those people and others too, freedom waited across the waters of Lake Michigan and Lake Huron.

For them, the Underground Railroad was not a "freedom train," but a "freedom ship," making the journey from the ports of Wisconsin to Canada.

These are the routes most commonly followed by steamships smuggling fugitive slaves to freedom in Canada.

Chapter 9

Open Hearts, Open Hands

A thin, tired-eyed woman pried open a missionary barrel in the Union Army chaplain's tent. She ran her hands over little flower-print dresses and rough cotton trousers and whispered a prayer of thanks for the Michigan girls and women who had sent them. She could have used ten more barrels of clothing and still not had enough. So many fugitives had come to Fort Pillow, Tennessee, that

Laura Haviland wondered if every slave on every plantation in the entire South had run. But every day, more arrived.

One by one she pulled clothes from the barrel and
handed them to a long line of shivering children. Ragged
flour sack dresses and pants were slipped off, and clean,
bright clothes took their place. Suddenly, the tent exploded
with the squealing laughter of little
girls. Years later Laura
Haviland still recalled that
joyful scene.

"One little girl ex-
claimed in surprise,
'Oh, Milla, my dress
has a pocket, and see
what I found,' as she
drew out a rag doll two
inches long. Then a dozen
other little girls . . . found
similar treasures. . . . All were
on tip-toe with excitement."[18]

A s the Civil War heated up and Union troops pushed
further and further south, slaves ran away by the

thousands. Groups of one or two, whole families, or even all the slaves on entire plantations fled to freedom.

These refugees from slavery were ragged, hungry, and tired. After waiting all their lives to be free, the sight of Union-blue uniforms and the Stars and Stripes flying overhead drew them like a candle in a long, dark tunnel.

Fugitive slaves came not just to get help but to give it. Men said, Give us guns, and we will fight! They were willing to die for their freedom. When they were not allowed to fight, they dug trenches, cooked food, washed laundry, and hauled firewood. Some became spies, even returning to the South to learn secret information about Confederate plans.

But Union Army commanders did not know what to do with so many people. Food was so scarce that Union soldiers were stealing chickens and picking corn right out of the fields to feed themselves. How could they possibly feed hundreds and hundreds of fugitives, too?

Churches helped, sending freedom workers and supplies. Abolitionist women who could not fight slavery with guns took needles and thread and made clothing. And yes, Michigan girls really did stitch miniature rag dolls as a sweet surprise for other little girls to discover in the pockets of their new dresses.

Missionaries like Jeremiah and Eliza Porter, who had once hidden a father and two children in the church bell tower in Green Bay, Wisconsin, came as volunteers. Eliza nursed and cooked. Jeremiah and Reverend James Rogers from Fond du Lac signed on as chaplains.

James Rogers was put in charge of thousands of fugitive slaves in a crowded army camp in Cairo, Illinois. He had never seen so many human beings in his life.

"On Sunday just before sunset, over five hundred came in one body," Rogers wrote in his journal. Monday, "before breakfast was finished, another crowd of eleven hundred came to my quarters. It seemed as if the whole slave population were really fleeing."[19]

Contrabands Escaping by Thomas Nast, 1864. Northerners looked at Thomas Nast's stories and drawings in *Harper's Weekly* for news of daily life on the battlefront during the Civil War.

Open Hearts, Open Hands

Mothers with babies, orphaned children, strong men, and sick, old people lined up outside Reverend Rogers's tent. From sunrise to midnight, Reverend Rogers worked like ten men. An empty tent became a school where former slaves crowded together, learning to read. Wash boilers were hung over open fires to cook cornmeal or wild-rabbit stew. Every night Rogers collapsed on his cot, knowing more people would come in the morning. This could not go on!

In some camps the gates were barred, and hundreds of fugitive slaves sent away. We're here to fight a war, not operate a refugee camp, commanders grumbled. Some soldiers protested. They had come to fight slavery, not send people back to it. But orders were orders.

Abolitionists were horrified. How could the Union send innocent people back to slavery? Orders might be orders, but wrong was also *wrong*. Then they found a way around the orders using the army's own rules.

The orders said no refugees. So abolitionists decided fugitive slaves weren't refugees, they were *contraband*. Contraband was anything useful to an army, from corn in a farmer's field to blankets on the shelves of a general store.

Fugitive slaves were useful. The army was desperate for workers. So when orders came to turn fugitive slaves away, soldiers like Reverend Rogers refused. What fugitive slaves? Reverend Rogers only saw contraband!

Newly freed people helped the Union in another way. Reverend Rogers knew that back in Wisconsin, women and children struggled to keep farms running while their men fought as soldiers. In Illinois he saw thousands of former slaves ready and willing to work. Would people in Fond du Lac hire them? They would, and they did!

Plans were set, and people volunteered. Then, early one morning, 75 men, women, and children boarded a train in Cairo, Illinois, bound for Fond du Lac, Wisconsin. One of those children was 15-year-old Frances Shirley.

Frances huddled in the train car with everything she owned bundled in her lap. Before her family ran away, she had spent her whole life on Master Harris's plantation far away in Alabama. Now she was surrounded by strangers headed to an unknown place called Wisconsin. Imagine the questions tumbling through her mind. Was the North really filled with snow and wild animals like Master Harris had always claimed? Would she freeze ice-solid in winter? Would white folks in Wisconsin pay her to work, or would they just force her into slavery again?

On October 21, 1862, the train puffed into the Fond du Lac station. Outside, the leaves were golden, and the air was chilly. White faces peered into the windows of the train. Strangers. Some smiled. Others scowled and muttered. Frances saw supper laid out on long tables. Now she would find the answers to all those troublesome questions.

After supper the adults talked about jobs. Men were hired as field hands. Women found work as housekeepers or laundresses. Frances Shirley got a job as a "baby girl," helping Mrs. Gould with her little ones. Imagine, not long before, Frances had been stuffed in a train car in Cairo, Illinois, without a penny to her name. Now she had a paying job!

After the Civil War, Frances Shirley and her family stayed in Fond du Lac. She married, and her children grew up playing on Dixie Street along the Fond du Lac River and singing in the Freedman's Union Church choir. In 1935, the city honored Frances Shirley's 88th birthday. She lived to be one of the last people in Wisconsin to have been born a slave.

Chapter **10**

Fix Bayonets!

It was October of 1862. Flags waved and voices shouted as the 22nd Wisconsin Volunteers—the *Abolition Regiment*—marched through the streets of Racine. Everyone cheered. Sweethearts cried. Hats and white lace handkerchiefs flew into the air like pigeons on hunting day as the troops marched away. Every last soldier was a Wisconsin man. Colonel William Utley rode at their head, gold buttons gleaming on his Union-blue jacket. It was a proud day.

Everyone knew William Utley. He

was not a professional soldier, but his fierce loyalty to his men earned their loyalty in return.

Even in 1862, early in the Civil War, Wisconsin soldiers had earned a reputation as furious fighters. Wisconsin men died in nearly every place the war was fought.

Before the young men of the 22nd Wisconsin would march home again, they would fight terrible battles. All too soon Colonel Utley's men would become blood brothers with every other Wisconsin regiment, killing and dying.

Col. William Utley leads the 22nd Wisconsin across the Ohio River. Photo courtesy of the State Historical Society of Wisconsin, Madison.

The 22nd Wisconsin was ordered to Nicholasville, Kentucky, to train and drill and learn to fight. They were willing to fight, even to die. But they weren't willing to accept what they found in Nicholasville.

In 1862, Kentucky was like a patchwork, neither North nor South. Some folks fought for the Union. Others owned slaves and hated "Yankees." Utley's men grumbled as they set up camp in ankle-deep mud, scrounged for food, and slept on haystacks. But mud and growling stomachs were not the worst of it. Across the fence the freedom-loving men of Wisconsin's Abolition Regiment saw slaves working the fields!

Slaves? Most of Utley's soldiers were abolitionists. They were shocked. Wasn't Kentucky in the Union? Wasn't the Union against slavery? The grumbling became a roar. They had not left their wives and families to watch slaves work in the next field!

It was true that Kentucky was part of the Union. Abraham Lincoln *had* written the Emancipation Proclamation on September 22, 1862. However, his proclamation freed people held in slavery only in the states "in rebellion," *Southern* states that had left the Union. Also, the Proclamation didn't take effect until January 1 of the next year.

Kentucky was a loyal, Union state. It was also a slave state. What could President Lincoln do? If he freed Kentucky slaves, the state might join the Confederacy. The

Union could not afford to lose more states. In the end, the Union kept Kentucky, and Kentucky kept its slaves.

The angry roar of the Abolition Regiment was only the beginning. Soon, William Utley and his men would have to stand against Brigadier General Gilmore, the chief justice of Kentucky's supreme court, and the entire Union Army command!

A sign of trouble came one November day when a beautiful, light-skinned fugitive slave girl crept into the 22nd Wisconsin camp asking to see the commander. Wisconsin soldiers took her to Colonel Utley and listened in horror as she told her story.

The girl wept. She was only 18 years old. Her master had made plans to sell her to a man who bought beautiful, young girls to entertain the customers in his gambling house. The girl said she would rather die than be grabbed and pawed by drunken men. She begged the 22nd Wisconsin for help.

Colonel Utley and every Wisconsin soldier knew the brigadier general's orders. Hiding runaway slaves was forbidden. Fugitives must be sent back to their masters.

The roar of the 22nd Wisconsin became a thundering *No!* Orders or no orders, they would not let this girl be taken. "We came here as freemen from a free State, to defend and support a free government," said Colonel Utley. "We have nothing to do with slavery."[20] No one could order them to do slave catchers' work. Not even the brigadier general.

The girl's master stormed into the camp. He also knew the general's orders and demanded the girl's return. The men managed to hide her among the supplies. But with an angry slave owner on one side and the brigadier general on the other, Colonel Utley decided the best plan was to sneak the girl out of camp to a station on the Underground Railroad. So that's what the 22nd Wisconsin did!

About one o'clock the next morning, two farmers wearing civilian clothes whispered a password to the guards and drove out the front gate of the Nicholasville camp. The guards didn't look twice. Civilians often came to the camps. Maybe these two just stayed on for a bottle of whiskey and a late night hand of poker with some soldiers.

If the guards had looked closer, they might have seen something familiar about the driver and his companion. If they had searched the hay-filled wagon, they would have seen even more.

The two "farmers" were really soldiers from the 22nd Wisconsin: Sergeant Jesse Berch from Racine and Corporal Frank Rockwell from Hudson. As soon as the wagon rattled over the hill, a scruffy-looking "soldier boy" pushed out from under the hay. The wagon, with its three passengers traveled nearly 100 miles to Cincinnati, Ohio, straight up to the front door of Levi Coffin's house.

Levi and Catherine Coffin were peaceable Quakers. But

across the Union and even in Wisconsin, they were known as fierce fighters against slavery. Levi Coffin was called the president of the Underground Railroad.

Sergeant Berch, Corporal Rockwell, and the "soldier boy" dashed up to the house. In the daylight, anyone could see the "boy" was a mulatto with creamy-brown skin. Even in free Ohio they did not want to be seen.

Levi Coffin opened the door. From the entryway Berch and Rockwell could see guests chatting in the parlor. They nervously whispered a message from Colonel Utley. Then, as calmly as if strange soldiers from Kentucky knocked on his door every day, Levi Coffin offered Rockwell and Berch a seat and sent the "boy" upstairs with Mrs. Coffin.

Levi Coffin wrote the rest of the story in his journal. "Next morning the soldier boy came down transformed into a young lady of modest manners and pleasing appearance."[21] A young lady? Of course! The "soldier-boy" was neither a soldier nor a boy! Colonel Utley's plan had succeeded. Back in Kentucky, that Lexington slaver was still searching for his slave girl. Let him search! Let him shout and complain about losing a $1,700 slave to those thieving Yankee soldiers. Let him turn all Nicholasville upside down, because Jesse Berch and Frank Rockwell had taken his valuable "property" to Cincinnati, Ohio, right under everyone's noses!

Levi Coffin wrote, "Not content with escorting her to a

free State, these brave young men telegraphed to Racine, Wisconsin, and made arrangements for their friends there to receive her."[22] Coffin drove the girl to the train station and offered his arm as she boarded the first-class car. "She was nicely dressed and wore a veil, presenting the appearance of a white lady,"[23] Coffin recalled. As the train puffed out of the Cincinnati station, Berch and Rockwell raised their hats in salute, knowing the young lady would soon arrive safely in Racine.

Friday night—more than a week since they had whispered that password and slipped out of Nicholasville—Berch and Rockwell returned to the 22nd Wisconsin. The minute they jumped from the wagon, cheering began. Soldiers hollered and tossed their hats into the air. To the men of the Abolition Regiment, those two Wisconsin farm boys were heroes.

While Berch and Rockwell were gone, the 22nd Wisconsin and other regiments like the 19th Michigan had taken in and hidden more fugitives. Colonel Utley continued to stand firm. No amount of threats or orders could force him to give up the fugitive slaves hidden in his camp. More slave owners, including the chief justice of Kentucky's supreme court, came demanding their slaves. Each time, William Utley refused. Each time his men agreed. They were freedom fighters, not slave catchers. And besides, they were *Wisconsin* men; they would not retreat!

Finally, the Kentucky politicians and slave owners hatched a plan. Reverend George Bradley, chaplain of the 22nd Wisconsin, wrote the details in his journal.

Regiment by regiment, the newly-trained troops were ordered to the battlefront. First, the 19th Michigan regiment was ordered to Georgetown, Kentucky. As they reached the city, 40 men with drawn pistols rushed toward them. Every fugitive slave in the regiment was taken at gunpoint.

Other regiments where fugitive slaves were protected were stopped. Every fugitive was snatched and dragged away. Finally, the Nicholasville camp was almost empty; only the 22nd Wisconsin was left. The army's plan was clear as a bull's-eye on the side of a barn. Divide and conquer. The army command and the Kentucky politicians figured one regiment alone could not keep slave owners from reclaiming their "property."

Orders came for the 22nd Wisconsin to report to the docks in Louisville. A friend took Colonel Utley aside with a terrible warning. Every fugitive slave had been taken by force from the other regiments. He said men in Louisville "declared they would die rather than let the 22nd Wisconsin leave the state"[24] with even one fugitive slave. Sheriffs, slave catchers, slave owners, and Kentucky politicians lined the streets of Louisville. The trap was laid, and the 22nd Wisconsin had been commanded to march straight into it.

William Utley had orders of his own to give. "Fix bayonets!" he shouted. Row after row of soldiers lined up in marching formation. Guns were loaded. Bayonets bristled like porcupine quills as more than 1,000 soldiers marched into Louisville. In the center of the regiment, armed with pistols, marched fugitive slaves.

"I hope there will be no forcible attempt to take [any]one," Reverend Bradley said. "If there is, *there will be music.*" What music? The "music" of war—drumbeats of gunfire and the cymbal-clashing of bayonets! The 22nd Wisconsin would not surrender a single fugitive without a fight.

At the sight of the bayonets, the crowd pulled back. Would that Yankee colonel really fight for runaway slaves? Would the Wisconsin soldiers really use those bayonets?

As the troops approached, one slave catcher made a grab for a fugitive. A pistol fired. Reverend Bradley wrote what happened.

"Snap went a cap! Fortunate for Mr. Slave Catcher that the pistol in the hands of the fugitive missed fire." Then the Kentucky men learned the 22nd Wisconsin would, indeed, use those bayonets. "A dozen bayonets converged to the spot where the slave hunter stood. Some evidently penetrated his clothes,"[26] Bradley wrote. That slave catcher could not get to the side of the street fast enough!

The Abolition Regiment kept marching. The crowd kept threatening and yelling. Guns and bayonets remained fixed

and ready. In the end, the *entire* 22nd Wisconsin marched on board a boat headed down the river.

What happened to the people in this story? The girl rescued by Sergeant Berch and Colonel Rockwell arrived safely in Racine. She married a young barber and set up housekeeping in Chicago.

Sergeant Berch became quartermaster for the 22nd Wisconsin. A few months after the troops left Louisville, Colonel Rockwell was badly wounded and sent home. Colonel William Utley was sued by one Kentucky slave owner for slave stealing.

One year later, the story of the 22nd Wisconsin was telegraphed across the entire Union by a New York newspaper reporter. "Surely, you brave men, who stood so firm at that time, as you read these pages, will rejoice," the report read. "You did well. The slave is now free."[27]

Weapons used by Wisconsin troops in the Civil War. Photo courtesy of the State Historical Society of Wisconsin, Madison.

Chapter 11

History, Legend, and Story

Stories. Don't you love them? Remember Paul Bunyan fixing flapjacks for breakfast—greasing a griddle the size of a football field with slabs of bacon tied to his boots like ice skates?

Paul Bunyan tales, flapjacks and all, have been told and re-told in Wisconsin. Although they might have begun long ago with a real lumberjack who cut faster, jumped higher, and lifted more than anyone else,

everyone knows they are not true. They are legends.

What about history? History is told and re-told, too. Over the years, the stories change until no one knows *exactly* what happened. People wonder if 100 fugitive slaves really boarded steamships in Racine. Maybe it was 500. Or more. Did 1,000 people really smash the jail door with a battering ram to free Joshua Glover in Milwaukee? How do we know?

True stories, like those in this book, are *history*. Historians have the exciting but challenging job of deciding what is history and what is not. Underground Railroad history is especially challenging because the secrecy needed to keep freedom workers and fugitive slaves safe meant that very little was recorded in writing.

All stories in this book were told in writing. Some were recorded in books and newspapers. For example, newspapers reported Joshua Glover's rescue.

Some stories were saved in diaries or books called *memoirs*—collections of memories. From an army chaplain's memoirs we know Colonel William Utley shouted, "Fix bayonets!" as the 22nd Wisconsin marched through Louisville with fugitive slaves in the center of the regiment.

History is sometimes recorded in letters. Historians know at least 100 fugitive slaves escaped from Racine because A.P. Dutton wrote about it in a letter.

In 1880 Caroline Quarles wrote her friend Lyman

History, Legend, and Story

Goodnow. Two letters, along with a third from Caroline's husband telling the story of his own escape from slavery, were tucked inside a box and forgotten. Then in 1998, more than 100 years later, Lyman Goodnow's descendants in Waukesha, Wisconsin, found them. Reading those letters is like meeting Caroline face-to-face. Her words reach across 150 years of history to today.

The past is also told through *oral history*. Unlike Paul Bunyan tales, which everyone knows are invented, oral history is true. Both teller and listener know the stories are important and pass them carefully to the next generation.

In some African countries all history was once preserved orally. Storytellers called *griots* were, and still are, honored as keepers of history. In the U.S., when slaves were not allowed to read or write, the practice of saving history through told stories continued.

American Indian people also tell history. Some stories are considered sacred. Some are passed by tradition from mother to daughter or father to son.

Written history is saved on paper, between the covers of books, and even in tin boxes. How is oral history saved?

Stories are told and re-told. Sometimes bits are forgotten, or details change, but the heart of the story remains. The story of Theodore Fellows bringing a fugitive slave to the Bristol Tavern was *told* for many years before it was written down.

One Wisconsin family has kept its history alive in a story about their ancestor, Samuel Arms, and his Civil War drum.

Toward the end of the Civil War, 12-year-old Samuel Arms was a slave in Georgia. One day his master's daughter hit him with a riding whip. He grabbed it. In the struggle Samuel struck the young woman. What had he done? For a slave to touch a white woman was unthinkable. His master would kill him. To save his own life, Samuel ran away.

At that time, war had turned Georgia into a battlefield. The land looked as if a giant hand had swept across it, crushing and uprooting everything. Soldiers died by the thousands. Refugees wandered hungry and homeless. One of those refugees was Samuel Arms.

Samuel was alone. Perhaps hunger brought him to the camp of a Union regiment from Pennsylvania. Perhaps he hoped the soldiers would protect him from his master. No one knows. But, as the Arms family remembers, an officer hired Samuel as a servant.

Samuel was bright and good with horses. He became the regiment's drummer and followed his employer to Pennsylvania after the war, taking his drum with him. Years later, he set out for the prairies and hills of western Wisconsin to work as a horse trainer in the pioneer town of Hillsboro.

History, Legend, and Story

Samuel Arms married Mary Roberts. They filled their small house with children—at least 12! Samuel told them how he escaped from slavery and had once been a drummer in President Lincoln's army. For many years he marched in the annual veterans' parades, setting the pace with a steady beat on his drum.

Today, Samuel Arms's story and his drum belong to his family—grandchildren, great-grandchildren and great-great-grandchildren. The drum is a symbol of his life. It is a symbol, too, of his family's history and of African-American people fighting for their freedom. The Arms family shared this history with all Wisconsin by lending the drum for exhibit at the State Historical Museum in Madison.

Photo courtesy of Mr. Edward and Mrs. Blanche Arms of the Samuel Arms family

Samuel Arms's story is not the only Wisconsin story about slavery, slaves, and freedom. Tales about the Underground Railroad are told all over the state—perhaps even in your community. Some are history. Some are legends.

How do historians know which stories are true and

which are legends? They become detectives, examining stories like an investigator examines clues. Historians ask questions, hunt for information, and fit clues together like a thousand-piece jigsaw puzzle.

Suppose someone said a house in your town was once an Underground Railroad station. How would you find out if that was true?

First, look for documents like old newspapers, books, letters, or diaries. Historical societies, libraries, churches, and families that have lived in your community since the 1800s are good sources. Your librarian can help.

Next, ask questions. Were accounts written by eyewitnesses? How old is the information? Did your town have an anti-slavery society? Are known Underground Railroad stations nearby?

Finally, interview community elders and members of 1850s-era families. Prepare for interviews by scheduling a date and time. Tell the person you will be asking about Underground Railroad stories. Bring a list of questions and a tape recorder.

When your detective work is done, put the clues together. If you're lucky enough to find documents from the 1850s or 1860s mentioning fugitive slaves, you'll know your town's story is probably true.

Suppose you find your town is ten miles from a known Underground Railroad station, and the old house in the story was owned by an anti-slavery society member. With this information, you can decide the story *might* be true.

If you just discover that an anti-slavery society met in the house, you do not have enough information. Sometimes historians just don't know if a story is true.

Finally, if you don't find any evidence, you can be almost certain the story is a legend, and your town was not an Underground Railroad station.

This book tells almost all that is known now about the Underground Railroad in Wisconsin. No doubt more stories are waiting to be found. The people who find them must be willing to dig like archeologists, think like detectives, and dream like storytellers. You can join the search for this important history; just follow the tracks of Wisconsin's Underground Railroad.

Chapter *12*

Looking Down the Track

From the earliest days of slavery in the United States, black people freed themselves. A few slaves won freedom by fighting in the Revolutionary War. Later, some worked extra jobs, saving for years to buy themselves from their owners. Still others earned their freedom with their feet—they ran away.

Many stories tell how slaves ran north, toward Canada. Actually, runaways headed in every direction. Some fled to the Western territories. They became pioneers or found safety with American Indian tribes.

No one knows how many fugitive slaves ran from the deep South to Mexico or to island countries like Cuba or Haiti. No one knows how many spent their lives hidden in the swamps and bayous of Florida and Louisiana.

A few enslaved people returned to their homelands in Africa. Some were helped by abolitionists who believed God had never intended black people to leave Africa. A terrible wrong had been done, and these abolitionists thought the only way to undo that wrong was to send all black people back to their rightful "home."

Some African-Americans agreed. Some just wanted to leave the United States and the pain of slavery behind. They dreamed of building a free nation in Africa where every enslaved person could make a new life. Others disagreed, saying they had never lived in Africa and considered themselves Americans. They wanted to live in this country as free citizens.

History also tells us that some pro-slavery people tried to force free blacks to "return" to Africa. Slave owners wanted the government to make free people leave their homes, jobs, and family members still trapped in slavery. The pro-slavery people thought if free black people were sent away, the slaves left behind would be easier to control.

No one knows how many people gained their freedom by running. No one knows, either, how many were caught and returned to bondage, or how many tried and died in the attempt.

Freedom workers were found even in the far South, hundreds of miles from the nearest free state. Stories are told of Quakers and others who forged passes, hid runaways, and told slaves how to reach the free North. Some abolitionists traveled south just to free slaves. Some free black people and former slaves like Harriet Tubman risked everything—their freedom and their lives—to rescue others.

The main routes on the Underground Railroad ran through Michigan, Illinois, Indiana, New York, Ohio, and Pennsylvania. How many thousands of people traveled these roads to freedom is a secret history will never reveal.

Wisconsin was a "branch line" on this railroad to freedom—a back-road track used by small "trains" and few passengers. Wisconsin's freedom workers needed as much courage as those on the more-traveled routes of the Underground Railroad, however. Here, small groups of trusted and trusting friends relied on each other to help runaways reach the lake and Canada-bound freedom ships. When money was needed, the same people contributed again and again. The number of stations and workers were few, so every hand and hiding place was needed.

Wisconsin's freedom workers may not have been many in number, but they were strong and determined. When arrest warrants and jail doors stood in their way, they knocked them down—sometimes literally! When slave hunters came sniffing around like bloodhounds, abolitionists found creative ways to outwit them. Attics and cellars were not the only stations; a sugar barrel, a tunnel, and a warehouse on the Lake Michigan shore became part of the silent, secret work of our Underground Railroad. Free black people and former runaways in cities like Milwaukee and Racine or farm settlements like Pleasant Ridge helped former slaves find work and a safe place to stay.

Wisconsin's Underground Railroad must not be forgotten. These stories of people with courage to stand for freedom have lessons for us today.

Remember Lyman Goodnow's words about Waukesha's freedom workers? "We were very radical in our views of right and wrong. We opposed bad men everywhere; supported all fugitive slaves who came to us, and worked like beavers for the right."

Remember Dr. Dyer, an abolitionist from Burlington, Wisconsin, who said, "Can liberty and slavery long dwell together? Which side shall we be on? Surely we will be for liberty."

Even in Wisconsin, a free state, people had to choose between right and wrong. They had to take a stand for or against slavery. Every person who stood against slavery took a risk. Friends or neighbors might become enemies. Customers might take their business elsewhere. Everyone who helped fugitive slaves risked six months in jail and a $1,000 fine, three years wages! Still, when the question was asked, "Can you help?" person after person said, "Yes."

African-Americans and Wisconsin American Indians took the greatest risks of all. Indian tribes were already being pushed from their land onto reservations. They risked more trouble with the government. Free black people and former slaves risked their freedom and their lives each time they helped a fugitive slave.

Fugitive slaves and freedom workers believed in the right of every person to life and freedom. Even today, even in the United States, those rights are not always safe. People must still ask, "Which side shall we be on?" If Wisconsin's freedom workers could speak, they would tell us to follow the tracks of the Underground Railroad. They would say, "Be for liberty."[28]

Notes

Chapter 1: Freedom Dreams

1. Drew, Benjamin. *The Refugee: Narratives of Fugitive Slaves in Canada.* Boston: John P. Jewett and Company, 1856, pp. 314-320.
2. Drew, p. 320.

Chapter 2: Independence Day

3. *A History of Waukesha County.* Chicago: Western Historical Company, 1880, p. 234.

Chapter 3: Strong against Slavery

4. *A History of Waukesha County.* Chicago: Western Historical Company, 1880, p. 467.

Chapter 5: Secret Service

5. Porter, Mary A. *Eliza Chappell Porter, A Memoir*. Chicago: Fleming Revell, 1880. p. 139.

6. Porter, p. 139.

7. Porter, p. 140.

8. Porter, p. 141.

9. Mathews, Edward. *The Autobiography of the Rev. E. Mathews.* New York: The American Baptist Free Mission Society, 1866, p. 117.

Chapter 6: Overground, Underground

10. Foote, Eliza. Letter, "Fiftieth Anniversary of the First Congregational Church, Janesville, Wisc." (1895), p. 85. (All Janesville quotes from Eliza Foote.)

11. Goodrich, Ezra. *The Negro Imbroglio in the Milton Lodge of the Good Templars.* Milton, Wisconsin, 1865, p. 15.

Chapter 7: Sketches from the Road

12. Wheeler, Arthur. *The Telegraph Courier,* Volume LIX, Number 40. Kenosha, Wisconsin, February 16, 1899.

13. Jensen, Don. *Kenosha Kaleidoscope: Images of the Past.* Kenosha, Wisconsin, Kenosha County Historical Society Publishers, 1985, p. 19. (See *Manuscripts Old and New, Vol. IV,* Kenosha County Historical Society.)

14. Bacon, William C. "A Story of the Underground Railway in Bristol," *Manuscripts Old and New, Vol. IV.* Kenosha Historical Society Collections, pp. 41-42.

Chapter 8: Open the Window and Jump!

15. Green, Jacob. *Narrative of the Life of J. D. Green, Runaway Slave from Kentucky*. Huddersfield, Canada: Henry Fielding, Publisher, 1864, pp. 32-33.

16. Green, p. 33.

17. Green, p. 35.

Notes

Chapter 9: Open Hearts, Open Hands

18. Haviland, Laura S. *A Woman's Life-work: Labors and Experiences of Laura S. Haviland.* Cincinnati: Walden and Stowe, 1881, p. 253.

19. Rogers, James B. *War Pictures.* Chicago: Church and Goodman, 1863, p. 112.

Chapter 10: Fix Bayonets!

20. Bradley, George S. *The Star Corps; or, Notes of an Army Chaplain, During Sherman's Famous "March to the Sea."* Milwaukee, Wisconsin: Jermain and Brightman Printers, 1865, p. 74.

21. Coffin, Levi. *Reminiscences of Levi Coffin: The Reputed President of the Underground Railroad [1876].* New York: Augustus M. Kelley Publishers, 1968, p. 607.

22. Coffin, p. 608.

23. Coffin, p. 608.

24. Bradley, p. 77.

25. Bradley, p. 77.

26. Bradley, p. 77.

27. Bradley, p. 80.

Chapter 12: Looking Down the Track

28. Dyer, Edward G. Burlington, Wisconsin: Dyer Family Papers collection, undated.

To Learn More

If you want to learn more about the stories in *Freedom Train North*, the following sources will be useful. All books can be obtained through your public library via inter-library loan. Full bibliographic information can be found in the Bibliography.

Chapter 1: Freedom Dreams

The Refugees: Narratives of Fugitive Slaves in Canada by Benjamin Drew is an entire book of stories told by people like William Hall who freed themselves from slavery by running.

To Learn More

Chapter 2: Independence Day

Caroline Quarles's story was told best by her friend Lyman Goodnow in the Western Historical Company history *A History of Waukesha County*. A short version is also in *The Underground Railroad* by Charles Blockson.

Chapter 3: Strong against Slavery

The Underground Railroad by Charles Blockson and *Reminiscences of Levi Coffin* by Levi Coffin discuss who participated in the Underground Railroad and why.

The best source for Wisconsin's Underground Railroad history is *Negro Slavery in Wisconsin and the Underground Railroad* by John Nelson Davidson. A copy of this pamphlet can be requested through inter-library loan. Your librarian will find it in the Dane County (Wisconsin) System Collection.

Chapter 4: Jailbreak!

Read about Joshua Glover's story in the Western Historical Company history *The History of Milwaukee, Wisconsin, Volume II.*

Chapter 5: Secret Service

The whole story of the Porters and the family of fugitives is told in *Eliza Chappell Porter: A Memoir* by Mary Porter, or in Davidson's *Negro Slavery in Wisconsin and the Underground Railroad*, both available through inter-library loan. The Milton Historical Society website mentioned under Chapter 6 includes Eliza's own words about their experiences helping people running from slavery.

Chapter 6: Overground, Underground

Go on-line to find out more about the Milton House and Hiram and Eliza Foote in Janesville. At http://www.inwave.com/Milton/MiltonHouse/ you can also learn about Eliza and Jeremiah Porter, Joshua Glover, and Caroline Quarles, about routes and stops on the Underground Railroad, and how Milton House became Wisconsin's National Underground Railroad Landmark.

Chapter 7: Sketches from the Road

Some stories in this chapter are included in Davidson's *Negro Slavery in Wisconsin and the Underground Railroad*. To find out more about the Underground Railroad in any of the towns mentioned in this chapter you'll have to write or visit the town or county historical society. Ask your librarian or the State Historical Society of Wisconsin for addresses of local societies.

Chapter 8: Open the Window and Jump!

Jacob Green ran from slavery four times before he finally reached freedom. He tells the whole story himself in *Narrative of the Life of J.D. Green: Runaway Slave*. Your librarian can obtain a copy through inter-library loan from the Dane County Library System.

Chapter 9: Open Hearts, Open Hands

More information is available in the book *War Pictures: Experiences and Observations of a Chaplain* by Reverend James Rogers.

Chapter 10: Fix Bayonets!

The story of Colonel Utely and the brave 22nd Wisconsin is told in *The Star Corps* by Reverend George Bradley, *War Pictures* by Reverend James Rogers, and *Reminiscences of Levi Coffin* by Levi Coffin. In *The Underground Railroad*, Charles Blockson tells the young girl's story.

Chapter 11: History, Legend, and Story

To learn more about oral history, try *My Backyard History Book*, Little Brown Publishers, or *Celebrating Everyday Life in Wisconsin History* by Dr. Bobbie Malone of the State Historical Society of Wisconsin.

These books and other materials are recommended for further study of the Underground Railroad in the United States.

Nonfiction

Young Readers

Many Thousand Gone: African Americans from Slavery to Freedom by Virginia Hamilton. Knopf Publishers, New York, 1993.

Tales from the Underground Railroad by Kate Connell. Raintree, Steck-Vaughn Company, Austin, Texas, 1993.

The Underground Railroad by Raymond Bial. Houghton Mifflin Publishers, Chicago, 1995.

Older Readers

"Dear Friend": Thomas Garrett & William Still, Collaborators on the Underground Railroad by Judith Bentley. Cobblehill Press, New York, 1997.

From Slave Ship to Freedom Road by Julius Lester. Dial Books, New York, 1998.

Incidents in the Life of a Slave Girl by Harriet Jacobs. Harcourt, Brace, Jovanovich, New York, 1973.

Our Song, Our Toil, Michele Stepto, editor. Millbrook Press, Brookfield, Connecticut, 1994.

To Be a Slave by Julius Lester. Dial Press, New York, 1968.

The Underground Railroad by Charles Blockson. Prentice-Hall, New York, 1987.

To Learn More

Fiction

Younger Readers

Aunt Harriet's Underground Railroad in the Sky by Faith Ringgold. Scholastic Publishers, New York, 1992.

Escape from Slavery: Five Journeys to Freedom by Doreen Rappaport. Harper Collins Publishers, New York, 1991.

Meet Addy by Connie Porter. Pleasant Company Publications, Middleton, Wisconsin, 1993.

Minty by Alan Schroeder. Dial/Penguin Books, New York, 1996.

Sweet Clara and the Freedom Quilt by Deborah Hopkinson. Knopf Publishers, New York, 1993.

Older Readers

Lightning Time by Douglas Rees. DK Publishers, New York, 1997.

Listen for the Whippoorwill by Dave and Neta Jackson. Bethany Publishers, Minneapolis, 1993.

Second Daughter: The Story of a Slave Girl by Mildred Walter. Scholastic Publishers, New York, 1996.

This Strange New Feeling by Julius Lester. Dial Press, New York, 1982.

Other Resources

Cricket Magazine. February 1995 issue.
National Geographic Magazine. July 1984 and September
    1992.

Try searching these addresses on the Internet:
    http://www.ugrr.org/ugrr
    http://www.inwave.com/Milton/MiltonHouse/
    http://www.loc.gov/ammem/   (Slave narratives,
        Library of Congress American Memories Collection)

The Underground Railroad: Songs and Stories of Freedom by
    Kim and Reggie Harris. Chatham Hill Games, Phone:
    800-554-3039. CD, Audiotape, and video on UGRR
    history. Board game.

Bibliography

This list includes all sources used to write *Freedom Train North*. When a source provided information for a specific chapter, those chapter numbers are listed. Some sources provided general information about the Underground Railroad. Primary sources are noted by an asterisk (*).

BOOKS

American Memory. Washington D.C.: Library of Congress African American Pamphlet Collection; Daniel Murray Collection, 1820-1920.

Blockson, Charles. *The Underground Railroad*. New York: Prentice-Hall Press, 1987. (Chapters 2, 10.)

Bradley, G[eorge] S. *The Star Corps; or Notes of an Army Chaplain, During Sherman's Famous "March to the Sea."* Milwaukee: Jermain and Brightman, Book and Job Printers, 1865. (Chapter 10.)*

Coffin: Levi. *Reminiscences of Levi Coffin: The Reputed President of the Underground Railroad.* Cincinnati: Robert Clarke Publishers, 1880. (Chapters 9, 10.)*

Davidson, John Nelson. *Negro Slavery in Wisconsin and the Underground Railroad.* Milwaukee, Wisconsin: Parkman Club Publications, Number 18, September 14, 1897. (Chapters 1, 2, 4, 5, 7.)*

Drew, Benjamin. *The Refugees: Narratives of Fugitive Slaves in Canada.* Boston: John P. Jewett and Company, 1856. (Chapter 1.)*

Finch, Asahel. *Milwaukee Bar Association Meeting Records upon the death of General James H. Paine.* Milwaukee: Milwaukee Bar Association, 1879.

Foote, Eliza. *The 50ᵗʰ Anniversary of the First Congregational Church, Janesville, Wis.* Janesville, Wisconsin: First Congregational Church, 1895. (Chapter 6.)*

The Fugitive Slave Law and its Victims, Anti-slavery Tracts, No. 15. New York: American Anti-slavery Society, 1861.

Green, Jacob. *Narrative of the Life of J.D. Green, A Runaway Slave from Kentucky.* Huddersfield, Canada, Pack Horse Yard: Henry Fielding, Publisher, 1864. (Chapter 8.)*

Haviland, Laura S. *A Woman's Life-work: Labors and Experiences.* Cincinnati: Walden and Stowe, 1881. (Chapter 9.)*

Henson, Josiah. *The Life of Josiah Henson . . . As Narrated by Himself.* Boston: Arthur D. Phelps Publishers, 1849.*

Hill, Daniel G. *The Freedom Seekers: Blacks in Early Canada.* Agincourt, Canada: The Book Society of Canada, Ltd., 1981.

The Home Missionary, Vol. LXVI, No. 7. Chicago: Home Mission Society (Methodist), 1893. (Chapter 5.)

Howe, Samuel Gridley. *The Refugees from Slavery in Canada West: Report to the Freedman's Commission.* Boston: Wright and Potter Publishers, 1864.*

Bibliography

Kartak, Mollie Maurer. "Memories of My Childhood," *The Wisconsin Magazine of History, Vol. X.* Madison, Wisconsin: State Historical Society of Wisconsin, 1926-1927. (Chapter 7.)*

Leach, Eugene W. *The Racine County Militant.* Racine, Wisconsin: E.W. Leach, 1915. (Chapters 8, 10.)

Mathews, Edward. *The Autobiography of the Rev[erend] E[dward] Mathews.* New York: American Baptist Free Mission Society, 1866. (Chapters 2, 3, 5.)*

Noonan, Barry. *Blacks in Canada: 1861, Lists and Analysis.* Madison, Wisconsin: State Historical Society of Wisconsin, 1997. (Chapters 2, 4.)

Olin, Chauncey C. *A Complete Record of the John Olin Family.* Indianapolis: Baker-Randolph Company, 1893. (Chapters 2, 4.)

Petit, Eber M. *Sketches in the History of the Underground Railroad.* Fredonia, New York: McKinstry and Sons Publishers, 1879.*

Pond, J. B. *Eccentricities of Genius.* New York: W. Dillingham Company, 1900. (Chapter 7.)*

Porter, Mary A. *Eliza Chappell Porter: A Memoir.* Chicago: Fleming Revell Publishers, 1880. (Chapter 5.)*

Rogers, James B. *War Pictures: Experiences and Observations of a Chaplain in the U.S. Army in the War of the Southern Rebellion.* Chicago: Church and Goodman Publishers, 1863. (Chapters 9, 10.)*

The Sabbath Recorder. Janesville, Wisconsin: Seventh Day Baptist Church, 1854. (Chapter 6.)

Ward, Samuel Ringold. *Autobiography of a Fugitive Negro.* London, 1855. Reprint, Chicago: Johnson Publishing, 1970.*

REGIONAL HISTORIES

Current, Richard. *The History of Wisconsin, Volume II, 1848-1873.* Madison, Wisconsin: State Historical Society of Wisconsin, 1976. (Chapters 4, 5.)

The History of Milwaukee, Wisconsin, Volume II. Chicago: Western Historical Company, 1881. (Chapters 2, 3, 4.)

A History of Racine and Kenosha Counties. Chicago: Western Historical Company, 1879. (Chapters 2, 4.)

The History of the Burlington Plymouth Congregational Church. Burlington, Wisconsin: Burlington Plymouth Congregational Church, 1908. (Chapter 7.)

The History of Walworth County, Wisconsin. Chicago: Western Historical Company, 1882. (Chapter 2, 3.)

A History of Waukesha County. Chicago: Western Historical Company, 1880. (Chapters 2, 3.)

Jensen, Don. *Kenosha Kaleidoscope: Images of the Past.* Kenosha, Wisconsin: Kenosha Historical Society, 1985. (Chapter 7.)

Lyman, Frank. *The City of Kenosha and Kenosha County, Wisconsin.* Chicago: S.J. Clarke Company, 1916. (Chapter 7.)

NEWSPAPERS

The Advocate. March 1854—December 1860. Text-fiche, State Historical Society of Wisconsin, Madison. (Chapter 4.)

The Aegis. 2 March 1841. Text-fiche, State Historical Society of Wisconsin, Madison.

The Milwaukee Daily Sentinel. March 1854—December 1860, Milwaukee. Text-fiche, State Historical Society of Wisconsin, Madison. (Chapter 4.)

Wheeler, Arthur D. "Father Deming's Great Work." *The Telegraph Courier.* Kenosha, Wisconsin: Kenosha Telegraph Courier Publishers, 16 February 1899, p 1. Text-fiche, State Historical Society of Wisconsin, Madison. (Chapter 7.)*

The Wisconsin Free Democrat. 16 September 1850—29 February 1860. Milwaukee, Wisconsin, Waukesha, Wisconsin. Text-fiche, State Historical Society of Wisconsin. (Chapter 4.) Contains some primary source material related to Glover rescue and Booth case.

Bibliography

MANUSCRIPT SOURCES

Dutton, Achas P. Papers. Racine, Wisconsin: Racine Heritage
Museum, 1901. (Chapter 8.)*

Goodrich Family Papers. Milton, Wisconsin: Manuscripts Collections, Milton Historical Society, undated. (Chapter 6.)*

Landon, Frederick. Fred Landon Papers, unbound. Canada: J.J.
Talman Regional Collection, D.B. Weldon Library, University of
Western Ontario. Text-fiche copy available as Fred Landon
Papers.

"Memoirs of Captain Theodore Fellows," *Manuscripts Old and New,
Vol. IV.* Kenosha, Wisconsin: Kenosha Historical Society, undated.

Olin, Chauncey C. "A History of the Early Anti-slavery Excitement
in the State of Wisconsin." Manuscript Collection, Western
Reserve Historical Society, Cleveland, Ohio. Text-fiche copy,
State Historical Society of Wisconsin, Madison. (Chapters 2, 4.)*

Siebert, Wilbur H. *The Underground Railroad in Wisconsin.* Ohio
State University, Columbus, Ohio, 1893. Copy in Rare Books
Collection, Library, State Historical Society of Wisconsin.
(Chapters 1, 3, 8.)*

Underwood Family Papers. Wauwatosa, Wisconsin: Collections,
Underwood Baptist Church, undated. (Chapter 3.)*

Copies of some source materials used in *Freedom Train
North* are available in the Julia Pferdehirt Collection, Ar-
chives Division of the State Historical Society of Wisconsin at Madison.

Acknowledgments

Many people made this book possible. The author thanks the WCR for support and careful input, Diane Barnhart and Dave Jackson, editor and designer respectively, who went far beyond their job descriptions and Neta Jackson, who was pressed into service as well.

Scholars, including Mr. Clayborn Benson, Ms. Kathleen Ernst, Dr. Leslie Fishel, Dr. Bobbie Malone, and Dr. Nellie McKay graciously served as the advisory committee for this book. Dr. Jack Holzhueter's support and expertise was critical at every point.

Also, students at Elmlawn School in Middleton and High Point Christian School in Madison read chapters and gave truly expert input. Thank you all.

Special thanks to Ms. Terry Biwer Becker, Waukesha County

Acknowledgments

Museum; Fred Burwell of Beloit College; Mr. John Ebert and Thomas Kuchenberg, Fond du Lac County Historical Society; Mr. Lance Herdegen of the Institute for Civil War Studies, Carroll College, Waukesha; and Mr. Chris Paulsen of the Racine Heritage Museum. Also, Mr. Robert Fuhrman and Mr. Don Jensen of the Kenosha Historical Society.

Thanks to Dr. Phyllis Tousey Fredericks, Ms. Loretta Metoxen, and Ms. Shelia Powless for sharing information about Wisconsin American Indian history.

The author salutes so many librarians, including Julie Chase of the Dane County Library system and the staff of Middleton Library, for invaluable assistance.

Copies of this book have been given to schools, libraries, and historical societies in every Wisconsin community. Sincere thanks to the Department of Public Instruction, Wisconsin Association of Non-Public Schools, Families in School at Home and other homeschool groups, the Wisconsin Library Association, and the State Historical Society of Wisconsin for distributing these books to their affiliates.

Thank you to the Waukesha family whose generosity kept the Quarles letters from being lost to history.

Finally, the author is deeply grateful to and for Mrs. Charlotte Watkins, great, great grand-daughter of Caroline Quarles Watkins, who treated the author like a daughter. Bless you, Charlotte.

Wisconsin Sesquicentennial Corporate Sponsors

This project has been funded in part by the Wisconsin Sesquicentennial Commission, with funds from the State of Wisconsin and individual and corporate contributors. We'd like to express our appreciation for the generosity of these corporations, and recognize their contributions.

Trailblazers ($250,000 or more)
AT&T
Credit Unions of Wisconsin
S.C. Johnson Wax

Founder ($30,000 or more)
ANR Pipeline Company
Blue Cross/Blue Shield United Wisconsin
Color Ink, Inc.
DEC International, Inc.
General Casualty
Home Savings
John Deere Horicon Works
Johnson Controls
Kikkoman Foods, Inc.
Kohler Co.
Marcus Theatres Corporation
Michael, Best & Friedrich
Midwest Express Airlines
Nicolet Minerals Company
Northwestern Mutual Life Foundation
Promega Corporation
Robert W. Baird & Co., Inc
Snap-on Incorporated
Time Insurance
Weber-Stephen Company
Weyerhaeuser
Wisconsin Central Ltd.
Wisconsin Power & Light Foundation
Wisconsin Public Service Foundation
Wisconsin State Cranberry Growers Association

Acknowledgments

Voyageur ($75,000 or more)
Firstar Corporation
Harley-Davidson, Inc.
Marshall & Ilsley Corporation
Outdoor Advertising Association
Philip Morris Companies:
Miller Brewing Company,
Kraft Foods/Oscar Mayer Foods Corp.,
Philip Morris USA
W.H. Brady Co.
Wisconsin Manufacturers & Commerce

Badger ($10,000 or more)
3M
Aid Association for Lutherans
Allen-Edmonds Shoe Corp.
A.O. Smith Corporation
Badger Mining Corporation
Briggs & Stratton Corporation
Case Corporation
Consolidated Papers, Inc.
Dairyland Power Cooperative
Edgewater Hotel
Eller Media Company
Fort James Corporation
Fraser Papers
Green Bay Packaging, Inc.
International Paper
Jockey International, Inc.
Jorgensen Conveyors, Inc.
Kimberly-Clark Corporation
Mann Bros., Inc.
Marathon Communications
Marcus Corporation
Marshfield Clinic

Freedom Train North

Modine Manufacturing Company
National Business Furniture, Inc.
Oscar J. Boldt Construction Co.
Pizza Pit, Ltd.
Rockwell Automation / Allen-Bradley
Rust Environment & Infrastructure
ShopKo
Stevens Point Brewery
Twin Disc, Incorporated
United States Cellular
Wausau and Mosinee Papers
Wisconsin Counties Association
Virchow, Krause & Company, LLP

Pleasant Fund for Children and the Herbert H. Kohl Foundation provided generous financial support specifically for the production of *Freedom Train North.*

In character as Underground Railroad station mistress Nancy Goodrich, *Freedom Train North* author and storyteller Julia Pferdehirt presents true stories of Wisconsin's Underground Railroad in schools and libraries. She also is available for author visits and student writing workshops.

Additional copies and classroom sets of *Freedom Train North* may be ordered directly from the publisher. Teacher resource materials are also available for in-class unit study and project ideas using *Freedom Train North*.

To purchase books or arrange storytelling sessions, author visits, or writing workshops, contact Julia Pferdehirt at Living History Press, 7426 Elmwood Avenue, Middleton, Wisconsin 53562; phone: 608-836-7426; or e-mail: history@chorus.net.